CW00400129

# The Buildings C. . . .----

A study of the development of Frome and its buildings
over a period of more than 1300 years

By Rodney Goodall,
Dipl. Arch. (Oxford), R1BA, MaPS, DCHM, ICHB, FRSA

With illustrations by G F J Russell LRPS, A R Yeates, Terry Cliss, David Partner
and the author

First edition published by Frome 1300 Publications, 1985
Second edition published by The Frome Society for Local Study, 2005
Third edition published by The Frome Society for Local Study, 2013
ISBN 978-0-9565869-5-7
Printed by: Butler, Tanner & Dennis
Front cover picture: St John's Church, Frome, taken by Mrs Ursula Voigt.
Back cover picture: A. R. Yeates

# CONTENTS

# PREFACE TO THE SECOND EDITION

The first edition of this book was commissioned as part of a series commemorating "Frome 1300", the celebrations which took place in 1985 to mark the first 1300 years of the existence of the town. (The date was chosen as the median between the possible dates defined in historical sources - it could have been six years or so either side of the year 685.) Although I had already assembled much of the required information time was short, and the first draft proved to be too short. The revised version as published needed much more polishing, and I see that in the foreword to the book I promised that when I retired I would try to produce a more comprehensive volume. Retirement seemed to be so far away then, but it is now upon me, and I am duly fulfilling that promise.

I offer this book not as an historian, but as an architect who has practised in the town for over 40 years, and who has had the pleasure of visiting most of the buildings described herein during that time. It is intended as an overview of the development of the town, and I have left much of the detail to be filled in by the number of real historians who have written so much about Frome. Most of the information in this book comes from their researches, and I hope that in the many footnotes and the bibliography at the end, their valuable contributions have been duly acknowledged. Their continued researches have enabled me to update much of the information given here, and I must express my deep gratitude for their work, and indeed their friendship, because most of the people I have quoted have become valued friends over the years.

In such a work as this it is not possible to make a detailed mention of every building in the town - or indeed every Listed Building, as there are over 500 of these alone! However, in the last edition, there were some serious omissions, including all of the houses in Bath Street, which were worthy of special attention! I apologise in advance to any owner of a Listed Building who does not find a special mention of his/ her house: it in no way implies that that property is any the less interesting than those which have received particular reference, although it could imply that less is known about that particular property.

It is inevitable that such a work as this embodies a great deal of social history - a great passion of mine anyway - and this gives much more interest to the story of the development of Frome. It also goes without saying that although there was a great temptation to include more pure architectural history, I have resisted that temptation in order to make sure that this work has a more general appeal.

In revising the text, I am aware of how quickly things change, and how much has happened in the last twenty years. As a result so much of the detail in the first edition is now "out of date". There is therefore a need to declare a "cut-off point" for this book, and it seems logical to make this the year 2000, although some later information is incorporated where practical. This will leave the way clear for someone else to take on the task of recording the 21st Century at some time in the future! I hope that the resulting book does justice to all those who, over the years, have played their part in the life and building-up of our fascinating town.

I can not close without expressing my thanks to those who have materially helped me in the preparation of this second edition. Firstly I must thank Gerry F J Russell of the Frome

Selwood Photographic Society. All of the illustrations in the first edition, photographs and drawings, were my own - and I am no great shakes as a photographer: Gerry has vetted the illustrations with me, and has replaced the least satisfactory pictures with those of his own, some of which were in his archives, and some were newly taken. His pictures enhance this edition of my work enormously, and I am very grateful to him. Secondly I have to thank Alastair MacLeay, who kindly read through a late draft of this book and pointed out one or two inconsistencies, errors of fact, and so on, and who also gave me some additional information. I must also thank my partner Ursula Voigt for letting me use her photograph for the cover of this book, and for her indulgence in letting me hide myself away in the rewriting of this book!

Rodney D Goodall

Frome/Innsbruck
2005.

## PREFACE TO THE THIRD EDITION

Sadly, Rodney Goodall died in June 2011. Over the previous year, we had been discussing the publication of a third edition of 'The Buildings of Frome' which would include some additional material together with minor corrections to the text, where new information had come to light.
I have tried to maintain his vivid style throughout.
On behalf of the Frome Society for Local Study, I would like to thank Rodney's children, Tim and Rachel, for permission to publish this third edition, Ursula Voigt for her help and support and Alan Yeates for his choice and expert improvement of the illustrations.

Alastair MacLeay
2013

**ST. JOHN'S CHURCH**
The site of St. Aldhelm's Monastery, founded c685 AD: mostly rebuilt between 1844 and 1866.
(A R Yeates)

4

# CHAPTER ONE

# THE RAW MATERIALS AND THEIR ASSEMBLY

Until the beginning of the 19th Century, the nature of buildings in any part of the country was very much determined by the availability of materials locally, and of the skills available for adapting such materials into building components. Additionally, there was the need for intelligent design so that the buildings not only survived, but created a pleasant environment. Such factors materially affected the shaping of any community, and Frome was no exception in this respect. The whole situation changed when a "day's journey" (the maximum realistic distance for fetching and bringing back building materials) no longer meant a horse and wagon trip to the nearest suitable source (usually a timber mill or stone quarry). Firstly, the arrival of the canal system meant that by 1800 the seaport of Bristol was no longer the nearest point where imported timber could be collected - it could now be picked up this side of Bath; and then in 1850 the Great Western Railway arrived in Frome, and things were never the same again. Welsh slates for roofing, the various new patent cements, and later on bricks and other components could all be unloaded in the sidings adjacent to Frome railway station. The introduction of the motor vehicle, ever improving, meant that the scope for importing materials became limitless.

To go back to the earliest days of Frome, the site of this new community was on the rocky slopes of a river valley running through Selwood Forest. This meant that the earliest buildings were probably timber-based, sophisticated in the case of the new Monastery of St John, or merely tepee-like structures in the case of the local populace. The Romans had been in this part of the country (with, of course, one of their major settlements at Aqua Sulis, or Bath as we now know it), but the nearest evidence of their occupation so far discovered is a Roman farm at Whatley, a possible glass manufactory at St Algars farm, and a possible Roman road along the lines of Gypsy Lane and Friggle Street. Doubtless their construction techniques were remembered by some, and it is not unreasonable to expect that Bishop Aldhelm, the founder of the monastery at Frome (who had travelled throughout Europe and had been to Rome), or one of his colleagues, was proficient in the construction of stone buildings. The majority of those living in the forest were primitives - not even Christians, according to early sources describing St John's as a missionary foundation - and their buildings would have been similar to the structures of primitive races all over the world. We should imagine their buildings to be constructed of roughly cut and dressed tree trunks or branches set into the ground, and meeting and possibly bound together at the top, roughly circular on plan, all clad externally with turves or bunches of vegetation. The centre of the floor inside was often lowered so that a hearth could be formed, with a natural seat all the way round. Such buildings may be seen in reconstruction at some of the open-air building museums such as the Welsh National Folk Museum, at St Fagans, near Cardiff, or at Singleton, near Chichester. (Either would make a good day's outing from Frome, and both have fascinating examples of buildings of many ages and types.) The Saxon art of timber building probably reached its peak at Cheddar, where the Kings of Wessex built a number of large timber halls, some of which have been excavated and duly written up by the archaeologists.

Tradition has it that St Aldhelm's Church of St John in Frome survived until it was replaced in about the year 1170, and so it is likely that any original temporary (and probably timber) structure was soon superseded by a stone building. Certainly other examples of early stone buildings associated with St Aldhelm (at all the stopping points on his regular journeys between Sherborne and Malmesbury, where he held positions of responsibility in both towns) survive, of which the most notable is the Saxon Church of St Laurence in Bradford on Avon, a day's journey from Frome in those times. Although the nearest workable stone comes from the quarries of the Bath area, Frome is situated on a bed of Forest Marble, a tough limestone which is not easily worked or carved, but which can be extracted in practical-sized chunks, and built up as rubble walling, either with mortar or dry (although in the earliest times it is probable that where faces of exposed stone existed, such as can be seen in Vallis Vale, frost action would ensure that there would be a supply of suitably sized stone all ready for use). St John's Church is built on a rocky outcrop of this stone, and much of the material could have been just picked up off the ground nearby. Forest Marble has proved to be extremely durable, and is one of the reasons why Frome has so many surviving buildings of interest. (It lives up to its name if a face is cut by a modern diamond-tipped saw and the surface is then polished - a beautiful marble-like finish can be obtained.)

There are a number of "grounds" or former quarries around Frome where this Forest Marble was extracted - on the Ordnance Survey maps of 1886 a number of small quarries are indicated, including one behind Gorehedge, two in Weymouth Road, and one each in Long Ground and New Buildings Lane which appear to be still worked at that time. Others were located at the bottom of Nunney Road, in Goulds Ground, and where Richmond Road now stands. Public works from the late 18th Century onwards would have also released supplies of good building stone (such as the cutting-through of the new North Parade at the end of the 18th Century, and Bath Street at the beginning of the 19th Century, and then later the construction of the railway and the gas works). As well as the main supply providing a good walling material, the thin stones at the top of the quarry could be used for roofing purposes, and stone slated roofs were once very common in the Frome area.

For more "polite" and sophisticated buildings workable stones were required for the quoins (corners) and around window and door openings, and these had to be fetched from further afield. Bath and Doulting stone types were usually employed (although the conquering Normans did not trust English stones for some while after the Conquest, and they imported much Caen stone as well as Tournai marble from what is now Belgium). The Doulting type has been worked in the village of that name from at least 1175[1], and is found as far east as Frome, and a quarry at Oldford providing this type of stone was still being worked by Messrs Sewards in the 1930s. Bath stone is available widely from the area to the north and east of the town, and Odd Down, Combe Down, Westwood and Stoke Ground (Limpley Stoke) were all within a "day's journey". (Bath stone was well known even in Saxon times over a large area, and large blocks were carried down to Salisbury - Old

Sarum - as early as the 9th Century; later it would be exported all over England and even shipped to France)[2]. There were other stones from relatively local sources used for special purposes: stones suitable for window cills or pavings came from Bulls Quarry (at Marston near the west end of the Frome by-pass), and as this became worked out pavings were brought up from the lias quarry at Keinton Mandeville. Pennant grit stone, used for the kerbstones as the roads were developed, came from Temple Cloud, about 15 miles away to the North-West[1]. Other types of stone were used once the railway was in existence, such as the better Bath stones from Monks Park and Box Ground, and occasionally Portland stone, another stone of proven durability, might be brought up from the South Coast. (Box Ground quarry was, by tradition, founded by St Aldhelm, and his church at Bradford on Avon has quoins from that source)

However, whereas the rich few might build in stone (and there was not much wealth around Frome apart from various religious establishments, including the monastery of St John!), timber was the more likely choice for ordinary buildings. Gradually, experience in working the various types of wood showed that oak was the best and most durable for making the frames of buildings; hazel, being flexible, made good wattle infill which could be daubed with cow dung or lime; elm was the most suitable for floor boards; likewise, thatch, made from reeds, was more durable than turves or heather; that water reed was stronger than wheat reed, and so on. All of these materials were in abundance locally. Some of the stones occurring in the Frome area could be burnt to make lime, but chalk, which is much easier to convert to lime, was available from as near as Warminster and Westbury.

Although there were supplies of clay suitable for making bricks at Rodden, the use of brick in Frome was rare until the advent of the railway. There is a mid-17th Century brick cellar vault in Trinity Street, and a solitary brick façade of the 18th Century in Castle Street (currently known as "The Keep"), but otherwise brick is only found in chimney stacks, where its performance is superior to that of stone (and even here, it is likely that many of the chimney stacks are replacements anyway). Likewise clay roofing tiles were available but not widely used before the 19th Century - in great contrast to the town of Westbury just 7 miles (12km) away, which is almost entirely of brick and tile.

From surviving buildings in the area (especially in Cheap Street) it can be seen that over a period of centuries the art of building using a timber frame reached great heights of skill in Frome, with results which compare favourably with those of East Anglia and the Welsh Marches. It also suggests that in secular and vernacular architecture the art of stone building was only generally developed insofar as it provided a sound, water-resisting base for a timber framed building. Perhaps the finest surviving regional example of a mixed use of stone and timber framing in the area is the 14th Century George Inn at Norton St Philip, six miles to the North-east of Frome. From the 17th Century onwards, however, timber framed walls tend to become less common, and even relatively humble houses (such as those in the Trinity Area, which start from 1665) are completely of stone. Timber framing continued to be used internally well into the 19th Century (it appears to have been considered that such a frame would strengthen a one- brick thick partition wall), and until recently one or two external examples of such a late date could still be found.

7

It is worth looking at the standard of construction of the Trinity houses, because we have so many examples remaining of this period (1665-1725 or so). Because the local Forest Marble was the usual subsoil, not far below the surface, foundations could be (and were) minimal. The main walls were built up in two skins bedded in lime mortar, partly dressed on the exposed faces, to an average thickness of 1'8" (about 500mm). The interior was filled with "muck" - small stones and a weak lime/ sand mix, which often never achieved the status of mortar. The window and door openings, and any external corners, were dressed in worked Bath or Doulting type stone: most of the windows were originally stone mullioned in traditional style. Dormer windows where they existed would be timber framed, often moulded to match the windows below (as at 7 Trinity Street or 26 Vicarage Street, from which an original example is now held in the Frome Museum collection). Although just a few years previously windows might have been unglazed (relying on waxed linen, which was translucent, or thin parings of cow horn set in lead cames - of which there is a rare survival in a house in Milborne Port, Somerset), glass was now available in smaller pane sizes, and so "leaded lights" were the norm, occasionally with a wrought-iron opening light. Outhouses would still be unglazed, with vertical timber bars set close together to permit ventilation but not entry. Shutters were often needed, but these would usually be internal.

The roof frame would have been assembled from substantial oak members, sawn at one of the local sawpits (such as still existed in 1886 in The Butts, according to the Ordnance Survey map): normally the frame would have been pre-assembled on the ground, the joints checked and components numbered, before dismantling and reassembling in situ. Joints were normally morticed and tenoned, and secured by oak pegs. The usual pattern was an "A" frame with butt-jointed purlins (and often windbraced), and often the feet were braced by the first or second floor joists, the collars being used as supports for a low ceiling. In the smallest houses intermediate trusses were not necessary, the purlins and a ridge pole being sufficient to carry the rafters. Often edge timbers, not perfectly square, were used, and as the supply of good oak dwindled, softwoods might be used, sometimes in pole form with the bark remaining. Where oak was used, it has usually gone rock-hard with age, and in modern re-roofing masonry nails are necessary to fix tiling battens. (Often the oak frame will survive for many years after the ingress of water, as was the case with Rook Lane Chapel after the lead was stolen from its flat crown.) The roofs would usually be covered with stone slates[4], although there was need for a resident thatcher in the town well into the 20th Century[5].

Internally, the ground floor would be no longer of earth or a mixture of clay and chalk (necessitating the use of reeds strewn over the floor which had to be renewed fairly frequently), but would be of stone flags, probably obtained from Marston. The flooring beams above were usually of oak, with elm boarding which would take a good polish if waxed: ceilings would usually be plastered, often with a moulded coving (not exposed as is today's accepted convention for older buildings - only the poorest buildings were left unceiled, and even then the wood would be limewashed, both as a protection against insect infestation and also to bring more light into the room). Sometimes the ceiling decoration went further: there are quite elaborately moulded and strapwork ceilings in 3 Cork Street

8

and some houses in Church Street, but the finest example was removed from a house in Merchants Barton in the late 1960s and re-erected in a house in Bradford on Avon. Early joinery was normally in oak (or occasionally chestnut), with elm used for stair treads and risers, but by 1700 softwoods were being widely used, not only because they were cheaper, but they were easier to work, especially if the timber was to be moulded or carved. The coarser grain was usually masked by painting (generally no more than limewash, which, actually served as a preservative). Walls would be plastered using lime, sand and animal hair; dung was often incorporated, especially on the inside and outside of chimney breasts, as it gave added fire resistance. The walls might be also decorated with limewash, sometimes tinted with an earth pigment: alternatively a primitive form of distemper would be employed (lime wash with an added binder such as egg-white or sour milk). Oil paints, with white lead fillers, were developed in the 18th Century - various pigments, often highly poisonous, might be used, but the range of colours was fairly limited, and there were no bright colours - green and blue were very expensive and not in normal use[6]. Occasionally wall paintings have been found: a mediaeval example was found in Lower Keyford, and a dated painting of 1693 was discovered in Selwood Road in the 19th Century. Some timber panels of 2 rooms in Melrose House, Whittox Lane, were painted with figurative subjects, probably in the 18th Century.

This all changed in the 19th Century, as the Industrial Revolution progressed, and in particular as the railways spread across the country, radically changing transport issues. Most obvious was the use of different roofing materials. Welsh slate (which had been exported to America by the beginning of the 18th Century)[7], now appeared all over Frome, appearing in lower Bath Street and Broadway right at the beginning of the 19th Century. A more colourful and perhaps more attractive alternative was the clay tile or pantile, which was brought up from Bridgwater or Wellington; more elaborate patterns, such as the double Roman or the triple-roll, followed and were widely used in the town. Sometimes terra-cotta ridges or finials were used, and clay chimney pots appeared in profusion. Very quickly the scene changed into the great variety as we know it today, particularly in the old town centre. Other components were brought in from elsewhere, but it was not until about 1890 that red brick became accepted as an alternative to stone rubble: economics and labour costs must have eventually led the local builders to change. Badcox Parade, of about 1890, was probably the first major brick façade (albeit with stone dressings) in the centre of the town (but some railway buildings and buildings nearby may pre-date this), and then Portway, Avenue Road and Wallbridge Avenue, all close to the railway, demonstrated that brick (usually a raw red colour) was here to stay.

Other changes of note in the 19th Century were the development of rolled glass manufacture, allowing glass pane sizes, and thus window sizes, to increase (and the glazing bars to shrink and decrease in number, eventually disappearing altogether); the development of cast iron and later steel components, and the introduction of a variety of cements which set quicker and produced stronger joints than the traditional lime mortars, of which Portland Cement rapidly became the favourite, and was in wide use by the middle of the century. The development of coal tar dyes brought new paint colours, but none was more exciting than the introduction of Brunswick Green in the 1820s - the first commercial

9

green - which became the predominant colour for external paintwork thereafter, and for the next 100 years or so! Standardisation of components, especially window frames in both timber and metal, meant a change in the character of industrial and housing developments in the town: one only has to compare, say Castle Street or Selwood Road with Alexandra Road or Avenue Road to appreciate the effect.

Of course, even greater changes were to occur in the 20th Century. Apart from the increasing standardisation of components (and even whole buildings) probably the biggest change to affect Frome was the use of concrete in its many forms. Fortunately, there are not many buildings which feature bare concrete, but in the form of "reconstructed stone" (concrete blocks with either colouring or a facing of real stone dust) it has made a big impact on the outskirts of the town. This is really not very surprising, as such blocks are widely made in the quarries around the town, using the byproducts of their major material. Sadly, the material does not weather in the same way as does natural stone. Another concrete product now widely in use locally is the concrete roof tile, which is thicker and not so attractively coloured as its clay rival (and which likewise weathers differently). However, it is interesting to note how many of the new materials being used in building are proving to be relatively short-lived, and how we are repeatedly going back to using traditional materials for our best buildings! I am sure that this will continue to be the case in the 21st Century.

As far as designers go, however, much less is known about the Frome area. I have hinted that there must have been residual skills available locally as the legacy of the Roman occupation, and the religious community of St John's Monastery must have continued to build long after St Aldhelm had departed. Later work in St John's would have been under the direction of a master mason, a privileged class who travelled widely about the country directing the more important building works. The building of Longleat House (or technically a rebuilding after a fire in 1567), under the direction of Robert Smythson, must have had some effect on Frome, and it is most likely that many of the building workers on this project came from Frome. Certainly the small houses in the Trinity Area (albeit a hundred years or so younger than the earliest parts of Longleat) showed in their interior fitting-out that skills of both design and execution were learned from this project. By the early 18th Century there must have been several capable master builders in the town capable of proficient design, amongst whom we should number James Pope (builder of Rook Lane Chapel and the tower of East Woodlands Church), and there were also visiting architectural designers-cum-builders such as the talented Nathaniel Ireson of Wincanton. In the 19th Century architects came in from Bath (such as ffinden, Goodrich and Pinch), Taunton (Underwood, County Surveyor, and later Giles), Warminster (Stent) and from even further afield - Sir Jeffry Wyatt (or Wyattville, as he sometimes styled himself), then restoring Longleat House, for instance. Towards the end of the 19th Century Frome had its own architects practising in the town (the profession of architect was formally recognised in 1834), including Joseph Chapman jr (a mason who later dropped the title of "architect"), J. Ace Benyon and W. George Brown. In the 20th Century, Percy Rigg arrived in Frome about 1905, his practice being taken over by Ronald Vallis in the 1930s (now Nugent Vallis Brierley), and Lou Webb and J Coles practised as surveyors in the first half of the century. G Wheeler was in practice as an architect after the Second World War, and I set up my own practice in 1968, to be followed by several others, so that the town is now well served by professional designers.

10

FOOTNOTES

1. Alex Clifton-Taylor: "The Pattern of English Building": Faber, 1972.

2. Kenneth Hudson: "The Fashionable Stone": Adams & Dart, Bath, 1971.

3. Eunice Overend: "The Blue House Restored" (article therein): Blue House Appeal Committee, 1965, and also her "The Geology of the Frome Area", Frome 1300 Publications 1985

4. Royal Commission on Historical Monuments: "The Trinity Area of Frome": HMSO 1981

5. Frome Almanack: I have almanacks for the following years in my collection: 1858, 1865, 1876, 1904, 1915 and 1923, as well as directories for 1923, 1933, 1949 and 1970-71.

6. For a broader outline of 18th Century building practices, etc (with a strong bias towards London and Bath), I would suggest reading "Building the Georgian City", by James Ayres (Yale University Press, 1998): a visit to the Building of Bath Museum, in the former Countess of Huntingdon Chapel, The Vineyard, Bath, is also recommended (James Ayres, the author of this work, was the founding chairman of this museum).

7. AC Taylor: Op. cit.

# CHAPTER TWO

# THE DATING OF FROME BUILDINGS

In the following chapters I shall be dating a number of Frome buildings, some being given a positive date, and some being assigned to a particular period, and it is worth pointing out how I arrived at some of this dating. The dating of buildings is rather like walking through a minefield - you never know when you are going to make a false move! Not every date will mean the same thing: in some cases, the date given is that on which the building is first recorded in the rate books, but this does not necessarily imply that the building was finished by that date. In other instances, the ascribed date could be the date of actual completion, the date of occupation, or of the public opening of the building; the date of the laying of the foundation stone is another possibility - here the year of completion is not always the same as that of commencement. When a building actually carries a date plaque, it need not necessarily refer to the date of erection: it could indicate the date of purchase by a family, or the date of the marriage of sometime occupants or owners, or even more misleadingly, the date of alterations to the building. As if this were not enough, it was not unknown for 19th Century building owners to add a date of two or more centuries earlier to give a false history to their building! Internal dating is even more difficult, because the variation of detail is even greater: it is not uncommon, for instance, to find two adjacent roof trusses bearing dates several years apart - are the dates those of the felling of the trees, of the sawing of the seasoned timbers, or the fabrication of the trusses, or their erection (indicating a pause in the building process), or what...........?

The pitfalls, therefore, are many, and in research for the writing of this book I have found conflicting dates given, sometimes by the same writer at different times, and not surprisingly I am guilty of the same fault myself. Fortunately, over the last 25-30 years much excellent research has been carried out and published, particularly by members of the Frome Society for Local Study and their associated group the Frome Historical Research Group, so that in many cases we can now be fairly definitive in our dating. However, research continues, and it is not unlikely that some of the dates given here may have to be revised as new information comes to light.

Normally a building can be dated from its particular architectural style to within a range of about 50 years, or rather less in the case of buildings after about 1850. However, it is easy to be deceived by the style of, say, the façade, because often Frome buildings are not what they seem. Until the 1970s, for instance, the whole of the Trinity Area was generally regarded as a 19th Century development, although the pattern of the streets was known to have been in existence by 1774, the date of the first known street map of Frome: indeed, even the name of the area is misleading: Holy Trinity Church was only constructed in 1837/38 - prior to this the area was referred to as Newtown. It was not until the leases of some of the properties in the area were closely examined by an archaeological group after the properties had been compulsorily purchased by Mendip District Council for demolition, between 1973-75, that it transpired that the date of development of the area was between 1665 and 1725, which gave the area tremendous national importance. Even so, a sizeable portion of the area was demolished before this was known - we must be thankful that some survived. Legal documents, such as deeds, leases, wills and surveys (including Parish Rate Books) are often the best guide to dating buildings. It is very rare to come across architect's drawings or specifications much before the beginning of the 20th Century (and these do not necessarily indicate the year in which a property was built).

Another factor which has to be taken into consideration is the tendency to alter buildings rather than completely demolish them and start again: St John's Church is probably the prime example of this (although the 19th Century rebuilding was fairly severe). Behind many apparent 18th and 19th Century façades are the remains of earlier buildings (a fine example of this is Fairlawn House, in Christchurch Street East, which had a "facelift" in the early 19th Century, whereas behind the façade are the remains of a 17th Century inn). Many buildings sit on earlier foundations: I once did some alterations to a shop in Cheap Street which seemed to be totally of the 19th Century, but its cellar and foundations bear no relationship whatever to what is above. How, then, should one date such a building? The different dates of construction need to be clearly defined. Sometimes one can date the alterations from incidental information: it is common to find that a building was substantially altered by a new owner, so that the date when a property changes hands can often give a clue as to when the building was altered. In one property in Gentle Street where the chain of ownership was known, it was possible to date several different internal alterations by this method, with a reasonable degree of accuracy. Another complication is the tendency of written records (in which newspaper articles are not exempt) to describe a building as having been "rebuilt", or even as "newly built" when in fact they have been restored or remodelled: the George Hotel has been "rebuilt" at least twice in the last two centuries, but the rear elevation still betrays the 17th Century origins of this building, which could well sit on mediaeval foundations!

One last point on the dating of Frome's buildings: in the past many historians have assumed that a provincial town such as Frome would be subject to a "fashion time-lag" of some 30 years or so. Whilst this might be true of some towns it is clearly not true of Frome. Although it was a working town, with no pretensions of sophistication, it kept up with the times very well. From the times of Aldhelm and then the Norman Conquest, through mediaeval times to Longleat, the Trinity Area, and the 18th Century development of Bath, Frome was subject to so many influences from close-by fashionable centres such as Wells and especially Bath that it remained in the mainstream of style and fashion itself, and indeed, in the case of the Trinity Area, Frome appears to have had the earliest ever known leasehold development, and so was a trend-setter in this instance! As I have hinted earlier, Frome landowners were quite happy to employ architects from outside the town to ensure that their building was up-to-date; sadly even at the end of the 20th Century there was an apparent reluctance to employ local architects on local schemes! In the humbler examples, craftsmen were quite happy to repeat in their own homes the up-to-date fashions that they were employed to use in the grander buildings on which they worked (many "Longleat details" could be seen in small Frome houses of the 16th and 17th Centuries, for instance).

# CHAPTER THREE
# THE EARLY DAYS, WITH THE DEVELOPMENT OF SAINT JOHN'S CHURCH

There is no positive information on any Frome buildings for the first 400 years or so of the town's existence, and so any comments made have to be speculative. As far as we know, there is no surviving building work earlier than the 1160/1170 rebuilding of the Church of St John above ground, and there has been very little in the way of archaeological excavation in the central areas of the town. The earliest fragments we have are thought to be the two stones with Celtic-style carving which are built into the base of the interior of the tower at St John's Church which most experts agree date from about the 8th Century, and which might have formed part of the cross almost certainly erected in Frome to mark one of the last resting places of St Aldhelm during the journey of his coffin from Doulting, where he died, to Malmesbury, where he was buried. Peter Belham in his book on St Aldhelm[1] advanced the theory that the foundations of the original Anglo-Saxon church may still survive under the present church, and he outlined the possible plan size thereof, but it would require a carefully detailed plan survey to see whether this is feasible. It is quite possible that fragments survive - in the relatively few churches which have been properly excavated the foundations of earlier churches on the site are often found, not necessarily in true alignment with the current church; in the case of St John's Church it is likely that, due to the nature of the site where there is little room for manoeuvre, if anything does remain it would be right under the present building. As I pointed out in Chapter One, thanks to the durability of the local stone, it was not always necessary to grub up previous foundations before rebuilding, and this site appears to be a rocky outcrop with very good bearing capabilities.

Because of their links, with a common foundation, it is most likely that the original Church of St John would have been similar in size and character to the Church of St Laurence in Bradford on Avon. This fortuitous survival is a testimony to the skill of the Anglo-Saxon builders and the materials they used. Both churches would have been constructed by monks of Aldhelm's Order: indeed it is unlikely than anyone else locally would have travelled abroad or even regionally to see such permanent buildings and to establish their method of construction. Aldhelm's own experience of the former Roman Empire extended through France, Germany and Italy (as we know them now).

It has to be a matter of regret that little survives of the 1160/1170 rebuilding of St John's Church. The two remaining fragments which we can attribute to this era are the archway in the west wall of the Lady Chapel, and the piscina built into the side of the north aisle near the entrance to the organ chamber, (and these have been somewhat restored). It seems that gradually all of the works carried out under the guidance of Cirencester Abbey (to which St John's was attached by this time) have been supplanted by subsequent work. The chancel, the 4-bay nave, the transepts and possibly north and south aisles were reshaped around 1280, and the Lady Chapel was added about 1350. St Andrew's Chapel and St Nicholas' Chapel were built in the first decade or so of the 15th Century, following the establishment of St John's Chapel in 1378, and then the nave was extended to roughly its present length, to be raised by the addition of a clerestory before the end of that century. We have to assume that the church of 1500 was not so very different from the church as we see it today, but we know from Vicar Bennett's book detailing the 19th Century restoration[2] that it is by no means an exact copy of what went before.

After the Dissolution of the Monasteries, it seems that St John's Church received little in the way of maintenance and repair for a long while, for we know that by 1744, when the Revd. Lionel Seaman was Vicar, the Parish Vestry was concerned about the state of the church, especially the tower and spire, and they resolved to seek the opinion of an architect/ builder: John Wood the Elder, from Bath, was approached but there is no record of any reply[3]- indeed, he was probably too busy with his developments in Bath. Subsequently it appears that an approach was made to Nathaniel Ireson, an entrepreneur from Wincanton who is known to have worked as an architect, mason, sculptor, potter and general builder. His reputation came from the rebuilding of the chancel at Bruton Parish Church, the Chapel at Redlynch, his own church in Wincanton, and much work at Stourhead for the Hoare family and also at Redlynch for Lord Ilchester. Ireson was obviously so little impressed by the condition of the church that he submitted a design for a completely new church (for which he was paid), but the conservative Fromians obviously did not care for the idea of a Georgian church, and the only reaction was to appoint a local builder, Henry Fisher to a contract in the sum of £1,150 to rebuild the tower and spire[4], but it seems that even this work did not proceed, certainly not at once.

We know that some work was carried out in the 1760s; during this period the east window was partly blocked to accommodate a new altar-piece, and an oval window inserted, but details are uncertain. The descriptions vary, and two early 19th Century drawings show a full east window of traditional pattern, so the alterations may have been purely internal. The next major change was the provision of a new west front under the direction of Sir Jeffry Wyatt, or Wyattville, as part of the "new south approach into Frome" as Bath Street was to become. Wyatt was working for Lord Bath, one of the Patrons of the church, at Longleat in 1814, hence the involvement of this architect who was later to remodel Windsor Castle for King George IV. To set off this new façade, the forecourt in front of the church was created, by the demolition of The Bell Inn and several small cottages, and the screen was erected along the street frontage. This last was erected by Joseph Chapman Senior, a local stonemason, at a cost of £136 - the whole west front to the church (presumably largely a "veneer") cost £231[5]. The west front was not to last long - Vicar Bennett was quick to replace it, declaring that "in mercy to the architect" no picture or new-fangled photograph of the previous west front should survive[6]. Until recently it seemed that Vicar Bennett had had his wish granted, but in the early 1990s a lithograph of "St Peter's, Frome" came to light. It seems that the front was very plain, very much in the simple style of the first parts of Christ Church (which was erected only three or so years later), with simple "Y-tracery" windows to the nave and aisles[7].

In 1840 the church building was in poor shape, and on the instigation of an eminent London solicitor, J.H. Markland (who had been an admirer of Bishop Ken and who had edited an edition of Ken's prayers), a fund was set up to improve the tomb of Bishop Ken at the east end of the chancel. Benjamin Ferrey, the Diocesan Architect, was commissioned to design a new canopy to the strange metal skeletal grille erected in 1711, and this was duly erected in 1844. There was so much money left over (presumably from Bishop Ken's admirers outside Frome, because the town was entering into what was probably the worst depression in its history, as the woollen industry locally had virtually collapsed), that Ferrey was able to oversee the restoration and re-roofing of the chancel, and the reshaping of St Andrew's Chapel[8]. In 1849 W J Stent, the Warminster and Frome architect, was commissioned to report on the remaining structure of the church, and he painted a very depressing picture, which Vicar Bennett was to echo when he arrived three years later. It seems that the introduction of galleries, necessitated by the number of worshippers attending the church in the early 19th Century, had accelerated the structural decline by weakening the walls and columns of the nave and aisles.

Bennett started his restoration in a strange way - he had all of what he regarded as the "liturgical essentials" sorted out before he started work on repairing the structure. He had all of the old box pews cleared out and substituted "open" pews; he relocated the pulpit (which had been set in the centre of the church, obscuring any view of the altar), removed the galleries which had been installed some time before 1800 (which had now become redundant, as by this time Christ Church and Holy Trinity Church had been built so that the former accommodation problems were not so great), and he installed encaustic tile pavings and steps in the sanctuary, having also had the churchyard on the south side levelled and terraced[9].

There was then a short pause before Bennett entered into the next phase of the works. In 1860 he engaged Charles Edmund Giles of Taunton (whom Thomas Bunn described as "the first person born in Frome to be brought up as an architect"). It came as little surprise that Giles' report on the structure was even more gloomy than that of Stent eleven years previously, and he stated that "the necessity for immediate repair is such that in a short time no repair will suffice". He estimated the cost of the necessary works to be between £3,500 and £4,000. Accordingly the restoration programme was resumed, but it was to take six years to complete. The Frome building firm of Frederick and George Brown was employed, and in the next three years the walls of the nave and north aisle were rebuilt and new roofs installed, and the north porch with its parvise room was added. The vestry was enlarged, as was St John's Chapel which was adapted to accommodate the rebuilt organ. (The organ apparently contains the pipes from an unidentified church elsewhere in the diocese.) The next area for refurbishment was the Cork Chapel, which had seen its last internal burial as late as 1856 when the Eighth Lord Cork died. Here the whole was overhauled, re-roofed, and reshaped as a Lady Chapel. During the course of this work a very fine wrought iron 17th Century screen was removed, which eventually found its way to the Victoria and Albert Museum: the present screen is the work of the local firm of J. W. Singer. In 1863 the south aisle, south arcade and south porch were rebuilt; and then the tower was underpinned and the upper part of the spire rebuilt, for the second time in 50 years or so[10]. The chancel arch was reformed, dormer windows inserted into the chancel roof, and the sanctuary and Bishop Ken Chapel pavings were replaced with costly marble

16

work. In his book, Bennett tells us that one marble used was a rare Cippoloni marble taken from a Roman building in Sicily (this is dove-grey with brownish-grey streaks), and that others came from Italy and Ireland[11]. Finally the nave roof was reformed and the west front was rebuilt (incorporating the former east window); and then a new north approach to the church (from the town centre and Cheap Street), incorporating the unusual Via Crucis - probably unique for an Anglican church - was made, all in time for the planned commemoration of St John's Day, 24th June 1866, when the church could be fully used again[12]. (As a slight diversion, I wonder what Carver, Giles' senior partner in the Taunton practice, thought about his colleague's demolition and replacement of the 40-year old west front: he was a former pupil of Wyatt, and presumably had some reservations about removing the master's work.)

What are we to make of the restoration - almost a complete rebuilding of the mediaeval church? There can be no doubt that the building was in very poor condition structurally when Bennett arrived in Frome in 1852 (apart from Ferrey's recent work). In Bennett's own words "every part of the church, from west to east and from south to north - became eventually an entire reconstruction[13]: not totally true, because the base of the tower was retained and underpinned, and some of the lower parts of the walls on the north side of the church appear to have mediaeval stonework (especially in the Baptistry and Lady Chapel); it is also safe to assume that much of the foundation work is of earlier date. Nevertheless, the church is essentially a Victorian re-creation by two Diocesan Surveyors, Ferrey and Giles.

What is important is that the work was finished to very high standards: Bennett admitted that some £16,000 was spent from the local appeal fund (raised by a very depressed township), but in addition many private gifts of furnishings, fittings, etc. were given, and the total cost was nearer £40,000 - more like £2,000,000 at 2000 prices. (By comparison, Christ Church, Reading, a church roughly similar in size to St John's, which I researched in the 1960s, cost £11,000 in total to build new and fit out complete.) Bennett died a poor man although there are indications that he and his wife had originally been well off, and it is likely that much of his and his wife's money went into the church rebuilding, which marks St John's as a significant monument to the Tractarian movement (of which Bennett, of course, was one of the leading figures)[14]. Giles had been chosen for the bulk of the work because of his "good old English work"; but Giles and Bennett between them made so many changes of detail when the different parts were restored that virtually everything of archaeological significance above ground was lost, although it may be argued that some of the early features, such as the variations in the nave arcading representing two different builds, were perpetuated.

As 19th Century work, the church is certainly very impressive, especially as there has been little in the way of alteration since. The most significant changes are the removal of the aisle pews and the painting-over of the stencilled decoration in the chancel, with some modifications to the original decorative scheme, mostly carried out in the 1960s. One of the main decorative features is the series of roundels above the nave arcades, with bas relief representations of the parables on one side, and the miracles of Our Lord on the other: apparently these were still uncarved in 1886. They are intended as replacements for a series of circular wall paintings discovered during Bennett's rebuilding, positioned in the spandrils of the arches: he interpreted them as being a pictorial record of the Creation[15]. The font appears to be of the 12th Century: it seems it was found under some rubble in one of the galleries in 1846: it may be a relic of the 1160/70 church. The pulpit, sculpted by Phillips of London, was the gift of a parishioner (unnamed) in 1859, apparently but one of several gifts from the same source[6].

The sculptured work in the church is one of its main glories, and the work of several 19th Century craftsmen is represented. The south porch carvings are by Ezard of Bath, who also carried out the tracery of the Lady Chapel windows, but elsewhere the statuary and ornamental work are by Forsyth of London. He was essentially a monumental mason whose memorials are to be found in a number of English cathedrals; it can only be presumed that he was a friend of Bennett from his days in Pimlico, where the latter had served before coming to Frome. No other church, as far as is known, bears so much of his work, which includes the whole of the new west front (inside and out), the Via Crucis, and the reredos to the High Altar, and it is his work which provides so much of the individual character of the church, as well as being his own magnum opus. The supporting carved work was carried out by Hurly of Taunton, presumably one of Giles's trusted craftsmen[17].

Whilst giving credits to those who worked on the church, it is worth recording that the marble floors in the sanctuary and baptistry were by Messrs Poole of Westminster; the stained glass windows are from several firms. Those windows in position by 1866 included the north aisle windows (telling the story of St John) by Hardman of Birmingham; the Lady Chapel and East window of St Andrew's Chapel by O'Connor of London; the South window of St Andrew's Chapel, the tower window, and (presumably the refurbishment of) the West window (formerly the east window) by Wailes of Newcastle, the baptistry window (now removed) by Lavers and Barraud of London, and the East window of the chancel was by Clayton and Bell, who also carried out the applied decoration to the chancel and nave walls and roofs[18].

Later additions include the South aisle stained glass, believed to be by the local firm of Horwood Brothers who worked from Bridge Street. The chancel screen and rood loft (the actual cross apparently coming from Oberammergau) were added in 1892 (featuring more brasswork by J. W. Singer of Frome); and the reredos of the Lady Chapel was given by a parishioner in 1923[19]. The nave altar was added during the refurbishment and cleaning of the church carried out in 1966. The small window in the South wall of the tower was replaced in 1985 with a work by Mark Angus of Combe Down to commemorate 1300 years of Frome (and St John's Church) history.

The whole adds up to a most impressive memorial to the founder of Frome and its principal parish church, St Aldhelm, and also to the Tractarian Movement, in which Vicar W J E Bennett was a leading figure. Not surprisingly it is now regarded as one of the three most important buildings in the town as recorded in the government's List of Buildings of Special Architectural and Historic Importance (see the Appendix for details of this List).

FOOTNOTES

1. Peter Belham: "St Aldhelm and the Founding of Frome": Frome 1300 Publications, 1984.

2. Michael McGarvie: "The Book of Frome": Barracuda Books, 1980, but also see the most vital source of information on the 19th Century restoration of St Johns: Vicar W J E Bennett: "History of the Old Church of St John, Froome": Penny, 1866.

3. Michael McGarvie: Op. cit., but also his "Light in Selwood": Frome Society for Local Study, 1976.

4. George Sweetman: "History of Wincanton": Sweetman, 1903 or 1904

5. Michael McGarvie: Op. cit.

6. Vicar Bennett: "History of the Old Church of St John, Froome": Penny, 1866.

7. The Frome Society for Local Study has a copy of this print. At Christ Church, only one window of this type still survives, at the west end of the south aisle.

8. Michael McGarvie: Op. cit.

9. Michael McGarvie: Op. cit.

10. Michael McGarvie: Op. cit., but see also his "Frome Through the Ages": Frome Society for Local Study, 1982.

11. Vicar Bennett: Op. cit.

12. Vicar Bennett: Op. cit.

13. Vicar Bennett: Op. cit.

14. Michael McGarvie: Op. cit.

15. Vicar Bennett: Op. cit.

16. Vicar Bennett: Op. cit.

17. Vicar Bennett: Op. cit.

18. Vicar Bennett: Op. cit.

19. Rowland Tuckwell: "The Story of the Parish Church of Frome, Somerset": B P C Ltd, 1946.

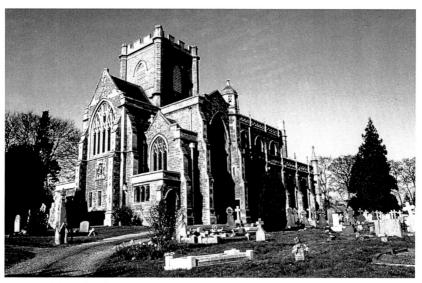

## CHRIST CHURCH, CHRISTCHURCH STREET WEST

The first daughter church to St. John's, begun in 1817 but not completed until 1929

## ST. MARY'S CHURCH, INNOX HILL

The second daughter church of St. John's, designed complete with church hall and vicarage by C E
Giles, architect for the St. John's restoration of 1863-64 (G F J Russell)

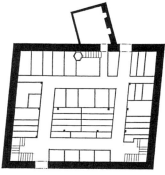

BADCOX LANE CHAPEL

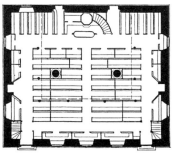

SHEPPARDS BARTON CHAPEL

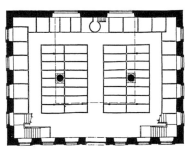

ROOK LANE CHAPEL

## COMPARATIVE PLANS OF THE EARLY 18th CENTURY
## CHAPELS IN FROME
All are to the same scale.

21

# CHAPTER FOUR
# THE OTHER FROME CHURCHES

Having described St John's Church, Frome's earliest-known and one of its major buildings, it would seem logical to proceed with an outline of the development of the other churches in Frome, before going on to describe the secular buildings in the town. I shall proceed in chronological order, which will reflect the rather complicated history of Christianity in Frome. The first religious building outside the confines of the Monastery of St John would appear to have been an oratory which Wandrille de Courcelles (then Lord of the Manor of Frome) was permitted to have in his house in 1156, although we have no details. It is probable that de Courcelles was responsible for the 1160 / 70 rebuilding of St John's Church. In 1253 we have the first mention of a Chapel of St Catherine, which was attached to the Manor of St Catherine[1]. Various arguments have been put forward for the location of this chapel: the site of Hall House (where the Westway Precinct stands now) is one suggestion, but there was no supporting archaeological evidence. The site has also been identified with The Old Presbytery, West End, but I feel that in this instance local tradition may be the most reliable indication: this has it where Nos 14/15 Catherine Hill stand now. There are certainly fragments of mediaeval work here, but there have been too many alterations subsequently to be able to identify which may have been the chapel, the manor house, the priest's house, and so on. These fragments include two corbel brackets to carry the raised crucks and arch- braces of roof trusses, with one moulded post in situ; there is a mostly concealed pointed arched doorway, and sundry fragments of early window surrounds (including some, apparently of 14th Century date, which were removed at the beginning of the 20th Century and are now in the Frome Museum). At first floor level there is a moulded plank and muntin partition which may be an indication of the post-Reformation conversion. There are also some semi-circular arches in No 15 which could conceivably be of 12th Century origin, but this would need opening-up for further investigation.

There is no record of any other pre-Reformation church building in the town, but, due in part to the liberality of the Thynne family of Longleat (who were principal landowners in Frome until the 19th Century) Non-Conformity flourished in Frome, and by the end of the 17th Century, at a time when Frome was expanding into the Newtown (Trinity) Area, various denominations were erecting their churches. The first group to build were apparently the Quakers, who erected a small building in that part of Sheppards Barton now known as South Parade in 1675. Their graveyard was alongside, and this survives as an open space between their former meeting room and Sheppards Barton Baptist Chapel. The original building survived until 1783, when it was replaced by the present building; however, the Quakers were never in a position to keep up the building on their own, and by 1856 it had been leased to the YMCA, and by 1879 it was doubling-up as a private girls' school. In 1933 it became the County Library for Frome, until larger premises were found in 1954. It was then sold to the local Red Cross Society, who used it as their headquarters and meeting room for nearly 50 years: it has recently been converted into offices[2]. As with all Friends' Meeting Houses, it was a very simple building, with a plain access stair and a gallery on the street wall: it was originally furnished with plain benches. After the 1662 Act of Uniformity, and the introduction of the new Book of Common Prayer (still the subject of furious debate after 350 years!), many local people broke away from the Established Church: not only did a large section of the congregation at St John's leave, but so did their Vicar, Dr Humfry. For some years the new congregation met in a local clothier's house. Rook Lane House, but finally, (after Dr Humfry had died and been buried in St John's Church) Rook Lane Chapel was completed in 1707. This Chapel, now regarded as one of the finest surviving Non- Conformist chapels in England, was built by James Pope (who also built the tower of East Woodlands Church for Lord Weymouth in 1712): Pope may well have been the designer as well. The original building was a plain rectangle of 7 bays by 5 bays, with internal dimensions of 18m x 12m (60ft x 40 ft). Internally there are two Tuscan columns supporting a 3-sectioned ceiling, of which the centre section was a domed vault which gave the church its local nickname of "The Cupola". Staircases to either side led to a gallery which extends around three sides; the building, lantern-like, was lit by semicircular arched windows at both levels on three sides, with two full length windows on the non-gallery wall opposite the entrance (see plan illustration). The main façade was all-ashlar, with a central doorway to the east front which was crowned with a broken pediment with flaming torch; the sides were of rubble stones with ashlar dressings. As so often happens, there were stresses within the congregation, and in 1773 some members formed a second Zion Congregational Church in Whittox Lane, an act which would mean the end of Rook Lane as a chapel almost 200 years later.

In 1810 the new "South approach to Frome" was formed to give what we know now as Bath Street, and Rook Lane Chapel benefited to the extent of gaining a new forecourt, garden and formal gateway (the previous forecourt was just 3.75m - 12ft deep). At some time between then and 1847 (probably c1835) there was a substantial remodelling, involving the removal of the stairs to the gallery (which was reduced in size, and given new cast-iron supporting columns) and relocating them into the present porch wings, which enabled the central doorway to remain closed (and later to be blocked up internally). A schoolroom was erected to the rear. In 1862 W J Stent, (a surveyor, auctioneer and valuer from Warminster who also had a Frome office for a while, and who also purveyed his own patent waterproofer), was engaged to carry out a programme of re-fitting to commemorate the bi-centenary of the founding of the breakaway congregation, which included the fitting of a new flat ceiling where the dome was, re-pewing, and the installation of cast-iron window casements in place of the (possibly decayed) timber windows. In addition, the rear schoolroom was raised (necessitating the partial blocking of the two long windows which now became circular), and further rooms were added. At the beginning of the 20th Century the roof was retiled, over the original very impressive oak frame. Sadly in 1968 the two congregations (of Rook Lane and Zion Churches) had so dwindled that they agreed to consolidate into one church, and as it had more space Zion Church was selected to be retained. After that, this splendid meeting- place (described in 1746 as being "handsome, perhaps, as any in England; and there are few more spacious") was left empty; its internal fittings were either removed or damaged by subsequent squatters, and it changed hands several times. Despite two programmes of repair works (firstly by one owner who intended to convert it into a house, and secondly by the Somerset Buildings Preservation Trust), the building had to wait until 2001 before it found a new use as offices for the architectural practice of Nugent Vallis Brierley, together with a public arts gallery and exhibition hall. The conversion entailed the removal of the 19th Century galleries and the provision of new accommodation to the rear, replacing very derelict 19th Century classrooms, etc; the future of the building now seems to be well assured.

In 1708, a year later than Rook Lane Chapel, the Baptists erected their first chapel in Frome, having been meeting for some years at the home of John Sheppard (a woollen mill owner) in Catherine Hill (which possibly embraced part of the mediaeval St Catherine's Chapel) thanks to a special licence granted to them in 1688. The new chapel was erected on land belonging to the Sheppard family in Sheppards Barton in what is now called South Parade. The pastor of 1773-1808, the Revd Job David, described it as being "better than Rook Lane, because it was beautiful on all four sides" (this probably referred to the fact that Rook Lane only had an ashlar frontage). A description of the chapel declared "it was 50 feet long, 42 feet wide and 30 feet high, with galleries around three sides. The ceiling was formed from the pillars, neatly ornamented with fretwork. The roof was sustained by two beautiful columns of the Doric order. The pulpit and sounding board were ornamented by excellent carved work. It had eight windows in the principal front, nine feet high, and in the back front ten windows. On each of its sides were four windows". In fact, this chapel was smaller than Rook Lane (see the illustration of the comparative plans of the 18th Century chapels) but so much resembled it that one suspects that they were designed by the same person. Alas, the building was demolished in 1849, and the present building (designed by J Davis) was opened in the following year, with the Wine Street schoolroom being added in 1852[3]. In its turn, the chapel was judged to be unsuitable for modern needs, and was closed down at the end of the 20th Century, and the schoolroom has been converted into flats. (Sadly, the one great feature of the chapel, the pulpit, which was almost certainly the sole survivor of the 1708 church, was smashed by the departing congregation to prevent it from coming into secular hands.)

The third of a remarkable trio of early 18th Century chapels was built for what must have been a rival group of Baptists in Badcox Lane (now Catherine Street) in 1711. The congregation of this chapel had been meeting in Hall House (formerly in Cork Street) since 1669. Due to a restricted site it was trapezoid on plan (see plan illustration), of double-roof style, 5 bays by 4 bays, with a side entrance. It had 2-light windows in plain mullioned surrounds, and internally there was a gallery on three sides carried on a ring of columns, with once again two central columns carrying the roof and valley gutter - generally similar in style to the other two chapels of this hectic building period. It seems that at first the baptisms were carried out in the river, mostly from Willow Vale, but in 1763 a baptistry was added to the rear. By 1813 this chapel was deemed to be too small, and it was demolished and replaced. The original Sun Inn next door was purchased and demolished to give a bigger site, and the new chapel (now converted into several flats) was opened in 1814. A schoolroom was added in 1845, together with a new entrance featuring the fine Doric portico which remains today (was this the inspiration of Thomas Bunn, the Frome worthy who was so keen on the Classical style?). In 1865 a lighting corona of no less than 60 gas lamps, costing £1,011, was installed; and in 1883 an 18th Century house which stood between the chapel and the street was converted into six extra classrooms[4]. In 1894 a beautiful series of art nouveau stained glass windows was installed. The chapel closed in 1962, and was sold to the Frome Urban District Council in the following year. From 1964 / 67 it served as the County Library, then it narrowly escaped demolition to provide a small car park. After a spell as a furniture showroom the building was converted into flats in the late 1980s.

The next church to be built in Frome was for the Methodists. John Wesley had visited Frome several times, and had preached in the Market Place, in the Pack Horse orchards (where Christ Church now stands) and on the Golden Knoll at Gorehedge. The Methodists' first meeting-place was in Behind Town (Christchurch Street West as it is now), between South Parade and Wine Street, and the site of the present church (Gorehedge) was acquired in 1779. Despite the handicap of the treasurer absconding with the funds raised for the first church, it was soon built, and Wesley preached there, but by 1810 it was too small. Accordingly it was demolished and rebuilt, using some of the materials of the original church. The works were carried out under the supervision of James Lester, and were completed in 1812. The building was extensively restored in 1871, following the addition of the major ancillary buildings of 1863 when the schoolroom, manse and other buildings in the attractive group on Golden Knoll were completed. The church itself, galleried internally, with a fine organ set in a large arch in the rear wall, is very severe in style, and its very plain façade is relieved only by a flat-roofed portico[5]. Major building works were carried out in the 1980's when the church was split in two horizontally: the church proper is now on the first floor, set at the lowest level of the galleries, and underneath a suite of meeting rooms has been created, complete with kitchen, etc., which has proved to be a well used facility, especially for ecumenical meetings.

The last of the larger churches in this group was erected in Whittox Lane with a later secondary pedestrian access from Catherine Hill, for a breakaway congregation from Rook Lane Chapel. There had been an earlier church on this site from at least 1773, possibly built for one Timothy Lacy, and the 1810 erection of this Zion Congregational Church is sometimes referred to as "a rebuilding". (It is understood that this first church stood nearer the site of the Sunday School building, according to a history of this church written by W J Harvey in 1918: it was demolished in 1837.) The church hall and other rooms to the rear are largely of this date, but the church proper received a drastic overhaul, and possibly an extension, in 1888. Here the designer and executor was Joseph Chapman jr, son of the monumental mason who had erected the screen to St John's Church forecourt, who for a while described himself as an "architect". He chose to employ a distinctly Northern Italianate style to the exterior, complete with ornamental gates and railings, including a secondary entrance to Catherine Hill: he may also have designed the attractive Sunday School building in the grounds[6]. This is dated 1875, and is an octagonal building with near-conical roof. Until recently it retained many of the original benches inside: it could not have accommodated many pupils. It is perhaps odd to create such a building when there were a considerable number of rooms available in the complex even before the 1888 extensions - but perhaps this was an early creche for younger children, whose exuberant noise might otherwise have disturbed worship in the main church! The building is now in separate ownership, and has been converted into a studio with an underground extension.

With all this activity within the Non-Conformist churches, what was happening with the Anglican Church? In fact it had been going through a very quiet time, largely because most of the town's clothiers were Non-Conformists, and in those times it was usual for their employees to worship in the same church: a census in the early 19th Century suggests that the Anglicans were outnumbered by their Non-Conformist brothers by a proportion of 4 to 1. It is an indication of the strength of the Non-Conformists in Frome that St John's Church had proved adequate in size up to about 1810, despite an increase in the population of the town. With galleries erected inside, it had been assessed as being capable of holding 1,639, many of whom were paying pew rents, so that there was not much room for the poor of the town. However, there seems to have been a population explosion in the town between 1801 and 1821, when the number of people living in the town increased by some 50% to about 11,000 (coincidentally its 1961 level). The arrival of a new Vicar in 1815 was the signal for the establishment of an appeal for funds for a new church, ironically a year or so too early to benefit from the national church-building fund set up in 1818 (the Waterloo Churches). The target figure was £8,000 which would have been enough to build a reasonable church, but as has happened so often in Frome, the funds raised were well short of this, and so a cut-down version of the original plans was built. The site was in the old Pack Horse orchards, (on which the pack horses had been allowed to graze after bringing coal from the mines at Mells and other locations towards Radstock, after being unloaded in the collier's yard behind the inn), and the church was dedicated as Christ Church. The architect for the original building was G. A. Underwood, a pupil of Sir John Soane, who by this time was County Surveyor of Public Works for Somerset: some of his other works include the Frome Town Bridge, Timsbury Church, parts of Shepton Mallet Gaol, and so on. A cruciform building had been intended, but when the church was consecrated in 1818 it had only a nave, eastern tower and north and south aisles, with galleries on three sides. It was fairly simple in style, with "Y-tracery" windows (similar to those on the west front of St John's at this time): one original window only still survives at the west end of the south aisle. The church had not been very well constructed, and the windows and their leading, in particular, soon gave problems: the organ was even worse, having expired after just 7 years! Manners and Gill, a firm of Bath architects, were called in, and between 1849 and 1851 all but the one window were replaced with larger, more Gothic styled traceried windows. There were also slight extensions westwards, and new parapets were added to produce a building more reminiscent of Bath Abbey. The church must have seemed less stark after these revisions: an 1853 engraving, however, shows that the tower was still left externally with three blanked-off arches which would have permitted the cruciform building originally planned. In 1868 William George Brown of Frome was called in to design more spacious pews (those which still exist), and to erect

26

a choir gallery at the east end, so that the west end gallery could be released for the use of the general congregation: the choir, now surpliced following Vicar Bennett's lead in robing choirs, was given a more prominent part in the participation of worship.

The church was still proving to be too small however (despite the building of two other churches by this time), and in the 1880s William Gough, a Bristol architect, was called in to advise on extending the church. However, he wished to demolish the tower, and his plans were rejected. After a new vicar arrived in 1894, William George Brown drew up more plans to extend the church. The chancel was re-arranged, choir and priests vestries constructed at the east end of the church, and in 1899 the south transept, housing a baptistry with the organ over, was added. The font was one from St John's Church, redundant after their mediaeval font had been found and restored. In 1904 / 1905 the east end was completed under the direction of Harold Brakspear of Corsham (who was later knighted), and the choir was relocated. A new stained glass window, by C E Kempe was added to the east wall; the previous window was to be later re-erected in the north wall of the Lady Chapel. In 1910 a new east gallery was built for the choir, which enabled closer liaison with the organist, but this gallery was removed in 1968 (and the choir still has no settled position in the church!). This work was carried out by Barnes of Frome, and after the interruptions of the First World War, which prevented a proper celebration of the Centenary of the church, the Lady Chapel was finally added in 1929 as a north transept (also to Brakspear's design), thus completing the church as it now stands. About 1960 a programme of re-ordering of the church began with the removal of the galleries to the aisles and rear of the nave, with near-disastrous results: a cast iron column in the south arcade was fractured during the process, and the church had to be closed as unsafe until all of the slender columns had been cased in concrete, rendering the once graceful arcades now one of the least attractive features of the interior. At the same time the church was wired for electricity for the first time (it was rewired in 1992)[7], and extensive decorations were carried out: these were renewed in 1990 / 1991, when the opportunity was taken to provide the nave, chancel and Lady Chapel with more elaborately decorated ceilings, and the plain shields in the nave clerestory were given detail for the first time.

In the 1830s church-going was obviously on the increase, and the rise in population meant that Frome saw a number of new churches during this decade: the need for new spiritual accommodation seems to have been particularly felt in the Trinity Area, as it is now. First was the Sun Street Chapel, opened in 1834 for the Primitive Methodists. This was a fairly conventional building with internal gallery, and a schoolroom and hall set at right angles on what was a very small plot probably achieved by the demolition of three or four houses; the plain elevations keeping a fairly low profile in an area of housing which had been established for 100-150 years. It was reshaped in the 1880s, and a porch added about 1910: it was closed in 1982 and part of the interior was stripped out, before the building was finally taken over by another Christian group. In 1835 a Baptist Chapel was erected in Naish's Street, but had been closed for many years, before serving as Messrs Paniccia's ice cream factory, it has now been converted into flats; finally in 1837-38 a new Anglican church was built which would give the area its name.

Holy Trinity Church was erected in the heart of Newtown by public subscription: the architect was H. E. Goodrich of Bath. Thomas Bunn, the Frome worthy whose diaries are an excellent record of the first half of the 19th Century in Frome, averred that Goodrich never saw the site, and that "the only requirement seemed to be that it looked well from the street"! The building certainly dominates the area, being set at the end of what was then Trooper Street and Cross Street, very much in the manner of some French cathedral: it looks enormous from a distance but the scale is illusory, and the double entrance doors prove to be quite narrow when you try to enter! In several ways this preaching-hall style church is rather un-Anglican; it is not particularly mediaeval in character, and is arranged very much as a matter of convenience for its users: the entrance is at the east end, consequently the altar is at the west end. Extending between the two corner turrets of the east elevation is a slim porch with gallery over; the remainder is an open hall with almost undefined sanctuary and a north transept which doubles as a baptistry, architecturally unremarkable. However, there are, in the tall lancet windows, some superb examples of the stained glass work of William Morris's friend Sir Edward Burne-Jones which redeem the interior.

Not to be outdone, the Rechabites erected a small chapel in Milk Street in 1840, but their style of worship obviously did not prove attractive to the locals, because it closed again in 1843. In 1853, however, the Irvingites established themselves in what is now known as the Old Presbytery at West End; later it was used by the Roman Catholics. The small building in which they worshipped still stands, more easily seen from Milk Street than from West End. In 1928 they moved to a new site in Park Road, where a "temporary" corrugated iron-clad church was erected (which now serves as their church hall). The permanent Church of St Catharine was erected in 1967/68 alongside this temporary church, to the design of Martin Fisher of Bath, who had been the writer's predecessor as assistant architect to Ronald Vallis.

The next chapel to be built was the tiny Bethel Chapel in The Butts, which seems to have survived until the 1950s or 1960s; this was erected in 1858. Two years later saw the erection of the Lock's Lane Baptist Chapel, but this closed about 1920. There was also a United Methodist Free Church in Catherine Street, which was built about 1851 / 52. By the beginning of the 20th Century the Salvation Army had a presence in Frome, and they appear to have used the Naish's Street Chapel for some years. Then in 1910 the United Methodists erected a new church on Portway, on the corner of the newly built Alexandra Road[8].

However, in concentrating on the Free Churches we have missed out the last of the Anglican Churches, St Mary, Innox Hill. This was erected in 1863/64 as another Chapel of Ease to St John's Church, and in conjunction with the major rebuilding of the parent church. Naturally Vicar Bennett employed the same architect, C. E. Giles, and the complex which he designed makes a very interesting contrast to that of the Wesleyan Methodist Church on Golden Knoll, erected at the same time. (Frome might have been undergoing a severe depression with considerable unemployment at this time, to such an extent that many of its population emigrated, but church-building carried on regardless!). The church itself is a simple cell with octagonal east end and fleche-style bell turret; there are lancet windows throughout, with a plain unplastered interior, but with a highly decorated sanctuary ceiling. The church is linked to a vestry, church hall/ schoolroom and a priest's house, making an imposing east-facing composition on rising ground. It became a separate parish in 1873, but merged with St John's Parish again before resuming its independence, but shared the same vicar as Christ Church in 2010.

This concludes a brief survey of the churches in Frome: before looking at the commercial and domestic buildings, it would seem sensible to look next at the various public buildings in the town.

FOOTNOTES

1. Peter Belham: "The Making of Frome": Frome Society for Local Study, 1973.
2. Derek Gill: "The Sheppards and Eighteenth Century Frome": Frome Society for Local Study, 1982.
3. Derek Gill: Op. cit.
4. Derek Gill: Op. cit.
5. Michael McGarvie: "The Book of Frome": Barracuda Books, 1980.
6. Michael McGarvie: "Frome in Old Picture Postcards" Volume 1: European Library 1983.
7. Derek Gill: "The Story of Christ Church, Frome": BPC, 1974.
8. Harvey and others: "Frome Almanack": volumes for various years.

## ST. CATHARINE'S RC CHURCH, PARK ROAD
Frome's most recent church, by Martin Fisher, of the early 1960s. (A R Yeates)

## THE BLUE HOUSE
James Wickham's replacement building for a mediaeval almshouse, of 1720-28.

## BRIDGE STREET/THE FROME MUSEUM BUILDING
North Parade, to the right, replaced Bridge Street as the main exit of the town northwards in 1797, The Frome Museum (formerly the Literary and Scientific Institution) dates from 1869. (A R Yeates)

## FROME BRIDGE
Probably the fourth bridge on this site, this is G A Underwood's contribution to Frome's new main through road, of 1821. (A R Yeates)

31

# CHAPTER FIVE

# FROME'S PUBLIC BUILDINGS

The aim of this chapter is to cover all those buildings other than industrial, commercial and domestic properties, which will be dealt with separately, and as before I shall discuss them in a roughly chronological order.

The first building (or structure) to come under this heading is the Town Bridge. It is almost certain that the earliest crossing of the River Frome for travellers along the old Ridgeway route between east and west was the natural ford at Spring Gardens; there must, however, have been a crossing not far from St John's Church once that had been established, and a site at or near that of the present Town Bridge seems the most likely. There has been speculation about a ford near this site, (possibly where the pedestrian bridge to the Westway Centre now exists), but the use of the island where the Blue House stands for a central bearing and support for a bridge would mean that it would not have been difficult to erect a fairly simple timber structure at this point. Today's bridge is at least the fourth: the first mention we have is from Leland when he visited Frome in 1540, when he spoke of a stone bridge having five arches. From a stone tablet set into the rear of the shop at No 4 The Bridge we read "This bridge was rebuilt at the charge of the County 1667, William Iveleafe, Richard Coombes, Surveiers". However, it is also recorded that when the Blue House was rebuilt in its present form in 1724 two arches of the bridge were rebuilt, but it is not certain whether the 1667 workmanship had been faulty, or whether the bridge had needed adaptation to provide a new access to the Blue House.

The next rebuilding (to give us the bridge as we know it now) was in 1821, when G. A. Underwood (the County Surveyor, who just a year or two previously had designed the first instalment of Christ Church), was charged with building a new bridge to complete the new road system through Frome. This had begun with the formation of North Parade (bypassing the old Bridge Street) in 1797, and had continued with the opening-up of the Market Place and construction of Bath Street from 1810 onwards[1]. In carrying out this work Underwood gave us a feature which is now nearly unique in England - a bridge with houses/ shops on it. The other two examples that are comparable are in Lincoln and Bath (although in the latter the Pulteney Bridge buildings are only single storey). The bridge is of stone with one wide elliptical arch for the main stream and two smaller arches on the market place side to take the overflow stream (as it is now) west of the Blue House, with a separate arch giving access to the Blue House itself. The houses, apart from No 3 which was largely rebuilt in the later 19th Century, were contemporary with the bridge, and were designed to match the classical style of the Bath Street terraces. The parapet on the south side has been removed, and a partially cantilevered footpath installed: this was done in the later 1960s at the same time as the river itself was modified to reduce the risk of flooding in the town centre, which had been a regular occurrence. (This involved the realignment of the river by the Westway Centre and also at Welshmill; and the river channels under the bridge and the overflow channel around the Blue House were given concrete beds.)

Frome's other river crossing, at Wallbridge, is nearly as old. A causeway was apparently constructed at the Wallmarsh at the end of the 16th Century, and the bridge itself dates from 1634. The area frequently floods, even after the alleviation measures of the late 1960s, and it is likely that the bridge has had to be repaired or even rebuilt on occasion. It is a 3-arch bridge with modern copings and railings. (The other river crossings in the area, Bradford Bridge and Murtry Bridge, are outside the area covered by this book. )

About 1621 there is mention of the rebuilding of the almshouses which had been founded by William Leversedge, Lord of the Manor of Frome, soon after 1465. This building consisted of a hall, a chapel and 12 chambers for old persons[2]. This lasted for just a century, because in 1720 James Wickham, a local solicitor and attorney-at-law, set up a public subscription for a second rebuilding, with the intention of incorporating a charity school for young boys (because by this time the 1540 "Free" Grammar School was only available for fee-paying pupils). The appeal proved successful, and nearly £1, 100 was raised which was added to existing funds, and by 1724 the new building, the Blue House as we know it, was completed, having cost £1, 401. 8s. 9d. The almshouse (the wings of the building) accommodated 20 old ladies, selected widows from the town; the school in the centre section catered for 20 boys. In 1728, not long before he died, James Wickham bought some land which generated an income which enabled the boys to be clothed and educated, in accordance with a Bluecoat foundation which gave the house its name[3]. The presence of both old ladies and boys was marked by two statues in the centre of the main façade: in her niche stands "Nancy Guy", and on a plinth in the broken pediment is the figure of "Billy Ball" - two traditional names for the statues, although the reason for them is long since lost. By the early 19th Century further endowments had been made to enable the school to take 40 pupils at a time. Eventually the school became a type of grammar school, and in 1921, after the State had taken over the principal role in education, Frome Grammar School (now Frome Community College) was set up at Northcote House, on the northern outskirts of the town; this took over the role of the Blue School and the latter was closed down[4].

Before we finish with the Blue House, however, we need to side-track a little to consider a parallel building. Richard and John Stevens, natives of Frome, had endowed further pupils at the Blue School, and when Richard, a leather-cutter and currier in London, died in 1796 he left money for the establishment of an Asylum to teach, clothe and maintain 40 local young girls of 7 to 10 years old, and for a "hospital" for 20 old men who were no longer capable of supporting themselves (subsequently 2 more men were endowed by the trustees of William Bayntum). Accordingly a new building, known as the Keyford (or Stevens') Asylum was built on what is now the corner of Culverhill and Stevens' Lane[5]. (It might well be argued that the old men, seeing these young ladies every day in their training for domestic service, came off rather better than the old ladies of the Blue House, who had to put up with typical schoolboys!.) The Asylum survived until 1957, (having doubled up as an army hospital during the First World War), when it was demolished. Because the school had closed at the Blue House, it became possible to merge the Wickham and Stevens Charities into a single Blue House Charity, and accommodate the old men in the Blue House. This building having been declared an Historic Building of National Importance, it was decided to improve the accommodation, and in 1963/65, after another public appeal, the Blue House was remodelled and restored in a form which would provide 18 flatlets for either men or women from Frome together with a resident warden. The links between the two foundations are marked in a special way at the Blue House: when the Asylum was demolished, two statues depicting young serving girls, which had stood in pairs in niches on the main façade, were salvaged and spirited away. They reappeared some years later in a Bath antique shop, and were rescued and brought back to Frome, where they now stand on a triangle of land beside the Blue House. In the late 1990s, further fund-raising enabled another refitting of the Blue House to be carried out, to bring the accommodation right up-to-date.

The architecture of both the Blue House and Stevens' Asylum was somewhat eccentric, and both took enormous liberties with what is known as "the scale" of the buildings: for instance the windows of the central section of the Blue House bear no immediate relation to those of the wings. To some extent the Asylum matched this, and it was probably influenced by the design of the Blue House. I have not been able to establish the designer of either building, but as the Blue House has a rather "amateur" feel to it one is tempted to speculate that James Wickham himself may well have indulged in what was a "gentlemanly architectural hobby" of that time, and designed it himself. It is certainly impressive, in its commanding position alongside the Town Bridge: the garden to the rear is also impressive, even after the walls of the old Town Mill, which stood at the bottom of the garden, have been demolished. (They were a picturesque backdrop to the garden, and were "Listed" for protection, but they went in the early 1970s.)

In the 1720s partial rebuilding of the Town Bridge in conjunction with the Blue House, there was apparently enough money left to provide a new guardhouse, or lock-up, in the corner of the Blue House grounds abutting the Blue Boar Inn (which had been erected by 1691). This replaced the old Blindhouse erected by the Parish (in the days when church and town parishes were synonymous) in the extended south-east corner of St John's churchyard. The position of this is clearly indicated by the double break in the churchyard wall as it abuts Blindhouse Lane. The Blindhouse was an underground stone- vaulted cell with stone slated roof, with a barred circular aperture for ventilation, and through which food could be lowered to the miscreant if the internee had any concerned friends or relatives. Amazingly, this 17th Century (or even earlier) feature still survives, having been excavated by members of the Frome and District Civic Society about 1980. It had featured in local tradition, and most locals refer to "Blindhouse Lane" even now, although the official name was "Church Lane": there was also a tradition that the Blindhouse had two cells, but the excavations revealed only one chamber, although this could have had a timber dividing wall long since decayed away. The 1724 Guardhouse was presumably made redundant when the Frome Police Station opened in 1857; at some time later it was converted into a men's public convenience, in which form it survived until the 1961/63 restoration of the Blue House, when it was demolished: some of the corner stonework may still be seen in the walling of the Blue Boar.

Another public building, first mentioned in 1727, was the Poor House, operated by the Parish Overseers for the Poor, and this was located at Welshmill. However, after the Poor Law Amendment Act of 1834 it became necessary to provide a new kind of building, and so a new Poor Law Board of Guardians was set up in Frome in 1837[6]. They very quickly arranged for the erection of the requisite new Poor House on open land on Critch Hill, to the west of the town. The building was "Y" shaped on plan, and was probably adapted from Samuel Kempthorne's "Panopticon" design of 1834, the more local architects for the scheme probably being Scott and Moffat[7]. The building had spacious grounds which were walled in; there was a small entrance lodge, and as well as having accommodation for paupers, there was a tramp's building, which provided stone beds in 7 cells, a stone table and primitive washing facilities. Having outlived the original purpose, the buildings became Selwood Hospital, a centre for the detention of the mentally impaired, but under the changes of the 1980s to give greater freedom to its inmates the hospital was closed, and the (listed) buildings were adapted into flats and renamed "Ecos Court". The site became surrounded by houses, and its entrance is now off the 1930's continuation of Weymouth Road.

At the end of the 18th and the beginning of the 19th Centuries a programme of public works was set in hand which changed the shape of the old town, and which was the primer for a whole sequence of building works which lasted some 30 years or so. The result was the Frome town centre almost as we know it today (with the exception of the Westway and the King Street shopping precincts). The basis of the programme was the creation of a new route through the town from west to east, to make it much easier for (horse-drawn) traffic to pass through. The other cross-route through the town, from Bristol and Radstock through to Warminster and Salisbury, had been developed on what was the edge of the town in the 1730s or thereabouts, and effectively bypassed the town; once known as Behind Town, and now known as Christchurch Street East and West, it eliminated the route from Badcox via Catherine Street, Catherine Hill, Paul Street, Palmer Street, Church Walk and either the now disappeared road south of St John's churchyard and possibly Vicarage Street (named Twattle Alley ) or up Gentle Street and along the Portway. The first length of the new cross-town route was North Parade, cut through in 1797, prompting the building of a terrace of houses on the north-west side which overlooked the town, especially Bridge Street, which it superseded to a great extent. Then the Market Place was opened up. Formerly two sections, Upper and Lower Market Place, it had been divided by a range of buildings extending from the site of the present HSBC bank premises across to within a few feet of the George Hotel and the Crown Inn, and it must have resulted in a serious bottleneck, and great confusion between pedestrian and vehicular traffic, even allowing for the much reduced traffic levels of those days. Included in the buildings demolished here was another inn, the Crown and Thistle. Then, in conjunction with the Marquis of Bath, who at this time still owned about one-third of the land on which Frome stood, another new road was created out of the Market Place to supersede the difficult route of Stony Street, Palmer Street and the right angle bend up Rook Lane to Gorehedge. This bend had been the cause of many horses and wagons coming to grief coming down the hill as their primitive brakes could not hold back the carts sufficiently for them to round the corner satisfactorily. The road also cut through a sordid backwater, Anchor Barton, which extended from Eagle Lane through into the yard of the Wheatsheaf Inn, branching out in both directions.

This new "South entrance to the Town of Frome" was illustrated in an engraving by Basier to promote the scheme (reproduced in the late Peter Belham's book "The Making of Frome")[6]. The instigator of the programme of works seems to have been a local worthy, Thomas Bunn, who deserves a biography sometime (although extracts from his diaries have now been published[9]): some of the more entertaining aspects of his life are given in Peter Belham's book. The whole of Bath Street, as the new road became, (much to the confusion of those visitors who assume it leads towards Bath - it was named in gratitude to Lord Bath, who gave the town the necessary land to create it and who is commemorated in the cartouche of arms on No 8 Bath Street, just below the church forecourt), was carefully designed and landscaped, in the classical style so much beloved by Thomas Bunn. The church forecourt had been cleared and the Wyatt screen erected, all as part of the scheme. The upper part of the street had nicely detailed stone boundary walls, still visible as the boundaries of Argyll House and Knoll House, but on the opposite side, to the cottages formerly in Rook Lane (the modern Rook Lane merely perpetuates the name) the lower walls are now nearly all below the pavement, as the made-up levels have increased over almost two centuries. One feature of the landscaping was the planting of two cedar trees brought from the Lebanon, paid for by Thomas Bunn: one died at the beginning of the 20th Century, but the other is still flourishing 200 years later[10].

As well as encouraging the new classical-designed buildings in the lower half of Bath Street, and the new Wyatt screen to the forecourt of St John's Church, Thomas Bunn was able to persuade the Earl of Cork and Orrery (of Marston Park, and at this time Lord of the Manor of Frome and owner of the George Hotel amongst other properties in the town) to provide two facilities which the town lacked. Bunn, who lived in Monmouth House, gave up part of his kitchen garden (across what is now Cork Street), and the Earl was able to erect an extension to the George Hotel (and, of course, suitably linked into it to ensure increased business!) which had a covered meat market at ground level and a large assembly room above. Bunn called this a "handsome room for public meeting, when we had no room except the mean one in Vicarage Street" - (presumably a forerunner of St John's Church Hall, possibly the then Grammar School)[11]. This was erected between 1819 and 1821, probably to the design of John Pinch of Bath, who is the signatory of some drawings held by the Frome Museum for Bath Street (I feel that it is much too "correct" to be by Wyatt, as Michael McGarvie has suggested). The Assembly Hall was the setting for many public functions, including, soon after it was opened, the local celebrations of the Coronation of King George IV in 1821, and the opening of the railway into Frome in 1850, with many other charity balls, dinners, public meetings, etc., right into the 1970s. The undercroft was only used as a covered market for about 50 years, being eventually superseded by the Market Hall of 1875; in the previous year the undercroft had been purchased by Stuckeys Bank, who converted it into an enclosed building and then moved in. This bank "drew on the London and Westminster Bank", and following a series of mergers over the years traded under the name of the Capital and Counties Bank, then the London, County, Westminster and Parr's Banking Company (which title was later shortened into the Westminster Bank), and finally, after the merger with the National Provincial Bank about 1970 it became the National Westminster Bank as it is today. Sadly, the George Hotel closed for business for about 2 years in the mid-1970s, having failed to "keep up with the times", and National Westminster took the opportunity to acquire the Assembly Room to enable them to extend their premises, and the fine hall is now sub-divided into offices - this loss of a public facility being a story repeated more than once in this book.

36

The next public building to be erected, in the upper section of Bath Street, was the first National School, opened in 1825 on land donated by Lord Bath. This was designed by another Bath architect, ffinden, in a very graceful Gothic revival style, but sadly its detailing was too delicate, and it ended its serviceable life strapped up with an inner steel framework. It closed down in 1934, having been superseded by the new St John's School around the corner in Christchurch Street East, but the premises were still used by the latter school for the mid-day meal until a new school hall and catering facility were provided in situ in the mid 1960s. The structure proved to be too frail to permit its conversion and adaptation, and so it was demolished in 1973, being subsequently replaced with the group of houses known as "The Maltings" (in deference to the brewery site which they also occupy)[12].

At the risk of affecting a smooth chronological sequence for the rest of this chapter, it would seem sensible to continue with the story of the development of the school buildings in the town. I will not deal with it in too great a length as Derek Gill has published a separate book "Frome School Days", a companion volume to the first edition of this book, which tells a more complete story[13]. The next of the "public" schools to be opened (Frome had a succession of private schools throughout the 19th and early 20th Centuries) was Trinity Church School, opened at the end of 1840. This was designed as an integral part of the church complex, but the name of the designer is uncertain - it may not have been Goodrich, as Thomas Bunn in his diaries states "Revd. Alfred Daniel is about to build a school; but seems to have as little knowledge of the affair he undertakes as his predecessor who built the church"[14]. This may, of course, have been "sour grapes" on Bunn's part if he had not been consulted about either project! I have always felt that this little building, with its obelisk finials, was very much like the sort of building a child would have constructed with his wooden building bricks which were as popular a toy then as they are now; certainly it must have been a very easy building for children to relate with. This school was doubled in size in 1887, when W. George Brown, the Frome architect was in charge. Originally it seems that the school was for boys only: a separate Girls' School was erected next door to Fountain House, in Gould's Ground, in 1854, but this was closed early in the 20th Century, and was demolished around 1970. The school buildings were closed in 1977 when the whole school relocated to a new site adjacent to Oakfield Secondary School (q.v.) on Critchill: the original section now serves as Trinity Church Hall, and the later section has been demolished to make way for new houses.

Then came the British School in Milk Street, which was set up in 1843, and occupied the premises of the Rechabite Chapel which had only been erected three years previously. Two classrooms, designed by Joseph Chapman jr, were added in 1875, and further additions were made on the other side of the playground in 1884 to provide an infants' school. It was closed for a while in 1894 to allow for further extension, and after the County Council took it over it was reshaped and further extended in 1909/ 10. The school and its premises still survive as the Vallis First School[15].

In the following year, reflecting the relatively sudden upsurge in educational needs, the Revd R. J. Meade founded and built, largely at his own expense, Christ Church School. He employed Sir George Gilbert Scott to design the school (one of a celebrated architectural family through several generations, of which the last, Sir Giles Gilbert Scott,

George's son, and architect of Liverpool Anglican Cathedral, died in 1960); Scott may have been working on Chantry Church at about the same time. However, his work was somewhat masked by succeeding alterations and extensions. A classroom and stairs were added to the rear in 1899, designed by W. G. Brown, and the unit nearest Park Road, with toilet facilities, second staircase, etc. was added by Brown in the following year. It became an infants' school in 1958 and a First School in 1973 when tertiary education was introduced in Frome, but it was eventually replaced by a new school erected on The Mount, on the southern edge of the town, which was opened in 1979. For a while the old building was used as part of the Frome Technical College facilities in conjunction with the main buildings opposite, but when this was closed down, in the early 1990s, the building was sold and converted into flats. The new school, which still includes, as do most schools in the county, some "temporary" classrooms, was designed by the Somerset County Council Architect's Department, and was extended about 1990 to include provision for a nursery class for the pre-school children, the first such public provision in the town; previously the only nursery schools were privately run in a variety of premises, and to date many of these still continue their work. The school has been extended further.

St John's Church, of course, had several schools associated with it. The principal school was the Grammar School, which was on the site of the current St John's Church Hall; but another school, originally run by Vicar Bennett, occupied part of Westbrook House (No 33 Vicarage Street, opposite) for a while before relocating to Nos 7/11 Wallbridge: this was a private, fee-paying school. The other schools associated with the church, as listed in 1865, were an Infants' School in Vicarage Street, a Girls' School in Church Lane (Blindhouse Lane), another Boys' School (adjoining the College), a Free School and House for Poor Girls, called St John the Baptist's Home (or was this another name for the Keyford Asylum?), a Free School at Innox Hill, and Woodlands School (East Woodlands)[17]. This group of schools seems to have been rationalised somewhat when substantial buildings were erected on the site of the present St John's School in 1875. This complex included not only a school and schoolmaster's house, but a soup kitchen and a dispensary. The site appears to have belonged to St John's Church for many years, and is generally thought to be the site of the vicarage prior to 1744 as well as the mediaeval tithe barn. Some of these buildings were apparently demolished when the larger part of the present school was rebuilt in 1932 to designs by H. A. Pictor, architect of Bruton and Bath; the remainder went when the school was remodelled in 1965/66 under the Frome architect Ronald Vallis: these last extensions were added to by Vallis and Vallis (as they were by then) in the 1970s. The sculpted bas relief of the lamb (the emblem for St John Baptist) over the main entrance was carved by Charles Hopkins in 1967. As far as I know, the only visible surviving fragment of the 1875 building is a small figure carved from a single stone which (if I remember rightly) stood over the doorway to the soup kitchen and dispensary, now standing outside St John's Cottage in the church forecourt.

About 1858 the Wesley Methodist Church built its own school, on a site to the south of, and above, the church, the buildings of which still survive as offices. A later schoolroom was added to the Golden Knoll complex (see Chapter 4) in 1863. The school was moved to a new site on Berkley Down in 1973, where there was need for another first school, and was renamed Hayesdown School. Another church school, which still survives in situ, although in more modern buildings, is the Roman Catholic St Louis' Convent School. This was started in 1861 in Conigre, probably in what is now known as the Old Presbytery. However, when the convent itself was established here, in 1902, the school was moved to Melrose House, in Whittox Lane. The sisters eventually sold the West End House and moved to Somerset Road in the late 1970s, (where they remained for a few years before they left the town altogether), but the school buildings, erected in the late 1960s on the West End site, remain in use.

As well as educational establishments maintained by the various churches in the town (until the County Council took over full educational responsibilities) there were a number of private schools in the town, a number of which (if the local directories are to be believed) were relatively short-lived. Education did not become compulsory for children until 1876, and there was no standard school-leaving age even then: most of the schools provided an education right through their school life (except for those who, after 1921, were fortunate to gain a place at the Frome Grammar School).

The County Council embarked on various educational building programmes in the town once it had assumed responsibility overall for education, some items of which have been recorded above. However, in 1938 it erected its first completely new school in Frome, Oakfield School on Critchill. Initially a school for all ages, it became a Secondary School under the 1944 Education Act, and then in 1973 became one of the town's two Middle Schools. (The "campus" of this school was later substantially enlarged in the later 1970s by the addition of the relocated Trinity First School, and the new Critchill School, a school for handicapped children, on adjoining sites, but these have access from Nunney Road.) The other Middle School, Selwood School, began as a Secondary School in the early 1950s, and was located on the Berkley Road out of Frome. The old Grammar School had relocated to Northcote House, on the northern edge of the town, in 1921: in 1938/ 39 the County Council built major school buildings on the site, and since the Second World War there has been a succession of new buildings, especially after the old technical college, erected in Park Road about 1900, became redundant in the early 1990s, (and was subsequently demolished), and the school changed into what is now Frome Community College, with a capacity for some 1,600 pupils, one of the biggest schools in Somerset.

To return to our sequence of public buildings in the town after our diversion into school buildings, the next development of some significance (although the local apathy of the time did not see it as such!) was the arrival of the railway, which was to mean a gradual improvement in the commercial fortunes of the town after the major depression which set in around the 1830s and lasted until at least 1865. The proposals of the Wilts, Somerset and Weymouth Railway Company to build a line into Frome were authorised by an Act of Parliament in 1845, but it was not until 1850 that the railway finally reached Frome, when on the 7th October of that year the railway station opened for business. In the meantime, the WSWR had been taken over by Brunel's Great Western Railway, and it was under the great engineer's direction that the station was designed by T. R. Hannaford in the office of J. H. Bertram, Brunel's close associate. The original design drawings are still preserved at Paddington, and they show how little the building has been altered since it was erected, even after a refit in the early 1980s and further repairs in 2000[18]. Few people had wanted the railway near the town, but John Sinkins, the clothier who lived at

Wallbridge (and who was to be a major contributor to the building of the Scientific and Literary Institution) was more visionary, and he sold to the GWR some of his land where the station and other buildings now stand, at a considerable profit[19]. In those days the station was almost "out in the fields" and was more or less equidistant from Frome and the old settlement of Keyford (by this time virtually linked with the town proper). Frome station, now a Listed Building of sufficient importance to attract two government grants towards its repair, (after becoming perilously close to demolition) is unique in the West of England in retaining its early form as a through "passenger shed" with timber frame and corrugated iron roof, with a simple row of offices on the town side in similar construction. One factor in the preservation of the station may have been that it was originally designed to take Brunel's broad gauge trains (2.15m- 7ft- wide instead of the later standard gauge of 1.5m- 4ft 8.5in), and so had a little more room to spare than later examples designed for the standard gauge which have now been demolished. Far more than the turnpike road system (and the canals which never actually reached Frome), the railway opened up an easy access for goods and passengers to and from Frome to the whole of the country. The fact that it took four and a half hours to reach London (via Chippenham) was a great improvement on the minimum day and a half for previous journeys: there were even four passenger trains a day in each direction then! The station was bypassed by an express line in 1935, but for another 40 years or so this line could not be used on Sundays!

Frome had been not a little unruly in the early 19th Century, with not only the well-documented 1832 election riot, but a weavers' strike in 1823, and several bread riots through to 1867. Consequently it was not surprising that as soon as the new Somerset Police Force was formed in 1856 a detachment of officers was posted to Frome, and in the following year the Police Station was opened in Christchurch Street West, alongside Wesley Slope. As well as providing a house for the sergeant, it provided cells and the Magistrates Courts (which latter had previously been sited in Justice Lane). The building may have been designed by Charles Davis, the Bath City Architect (who was also involved in the remodelling of Marston Bigot Church)[20]. The buildings were used for almost 100 years, until the new Oakfield Road Police station was opened in 1952, and then became offices and an auction room, before becoming a Dancing School and private house.

In 1858 the Mechanics' Institute building was opened. It was originally located in Catherine Hill (when it boasted a library of some 1,400 volumes), and was the location for various lectures and evening classes. It was not long before a new building was opened on the corner of Eagle Lane and Church Slope, and this survived until the beginning of the 20th Century[21]. The building later became a cinema (The Palace Theatre), and then part of an ironmonger's shop in Bath Street. It was destroyed in a serious fire in 1961, and replaced with what must be one of the most unsympathetic buildings in Frome, a brick flat-roofed building right in the heart of what is now a Conservation Area, spoiling one of the most impressive views of St John's Church.

This Institute had a rival, the Frome Scientific and Literary Institution, which had been founded in 1843, and which had Thomas Bunn as its first secretary. It boasted a reading room with 1,800 volumes, as well as a small museum. It was originally located in Palmer Street, and it was the intention that when Thomas Bunn died they should move into his house in Cork Street, but Bunn's will was declared invalid, and his heirs got the lot. (Bunn was qualified as a solicitor, but never practised: he should have left the task of drawing up his will to a brother solicitor - instead it ran to 85 pages, intending bequests for the good of Frome which in the event proved to be all in vain)[22]. It had been Bunn's hope that ultimately the Institution should have new premises on his land on the south side of Christchurch Street West (near the police station site) out of any remaining funds. However, another member of the Institution, John Sinkins, who had married into a wealthy clothiers' family, funded the now familiar building on the Bridge Street/North Parade corner. This Italianate building, which sits so well on an awkward site, was designed by J. Hine, one of Sinkins' relations, and it was finished in 1869, the year that John Sinkins died. Although the Institution survived until fairly recently, albeit as a social club rather than a learned society, its books were sold off over the years, and the original museum exhibits seem to have disappeared altogether. However, the Frome Society for Local Study founded a new Frome Museum in 1966, which was for some years located in Church House, on Church Steps, and then in Wine Street House, before being transferred to "The Lit Club building", as the Institution became more widely known, in 1985 - a lovely example of history repeating itself! For a while it seems that there was a third institution in the town aimed at improving the learning of the townsfolk: the Church Union ran a library in the Market Place, under the Revd W. J. E. Bennett as President, and with W. C. Penny, the local printer, as Librarian. This library is not mentioned in 1858; it was thriving in 1865, but seems to have disappeared by 1875.

The Frome Scientific and Literary Institution had formed a School of Arts in 1863, but by the end of the 19th Century this had grown to be too large to be accommodated in their main building, and so a new building was designed by the Bath architectural firm of Silcock and Reay, and was opened in Park Road in 1902. This became Frome Technical College, and soon absorbed the old Mechanics' Institute. The college was eventually taken over by the County Council, who more than doubled the size of the building with an extension in the 1950s, but the building was demolished in 1999; the Technical College (which had been merged with Radstock Technical College for some 20 years until the county boundary was altered) was merged with Frome Community College on the Bath Road site.

In 1863 an unusual building in the Egyptian style was erected in North Parade, and on October 29th of that year a Freemasons' Lodge was "consecrated, dedicated, and constituted into a regular Lodge of ancient, free and accepted masons" with the usual ceremonies, and was christened "The Royal Somerset Lodge of Freemasons". The design is credited to P Edlinger, but this may refer to an overhaul of 1891. The whole building still survives, albeit in a slightly modified form, its original use having been extended to include public functions in the downstairs assembly room whilst Masonic functions are still carried out upstairs.

In 1874/75 a Temperance Hall was erected in Catherine Street (where the small car park below Catherine Hill House is now located) to meet the needs of the thriving Temperance Movement of the latter half of the 19th Century, which, due to the strength of the Non-Conformist Churches in Frome, must have been particularly strong in the town. It was designed by Joseph Chapman jr (who had also designed the front of the Congregational Church in Whittox Lane), and erected by Thomas Parfitt of Frome, both of whom were teetotallers[23]. The hall was in regular use until 1954, when it was leased to the County Council as temporary premises for the County Library. After a fall of masonry in 1964 (probably the result of the serious winter frosts of that year) the building was declared unsafe, the library moved up to the Baptist Chapel schoolroom over a weekend, and it was hurriedly demolished. One of the features of its relatively sober façade was said to resemble a "teetotalling Hebe".

As a result of a new Public Health Act, in 1875 a hospital was opened in Frome for what was, seemingly, the first time. It was established in what used to be known as "Madam Castle's House" on the comer of Castle Street and Trinity Street, now known as "The Keep". It backed on to what was then the Butler and Tanner Printing Works - hardly a quiet area to aid recuperation! It was superseded in 1901, but despite being absorbed into the printing works campus, and being used for storage, the legend "Frome Hospital" could still be deciphered over the doorway, and the two wards (men downstairs and ladies upstairs, formed by gutting the interior of the main building and adding stairs, etc. to the rear) were still identifiable before it was reconverted into a house about 1980. The whole building is something of a mystery - it is one of only two houses of any substance in the Trinity Area (the other being No 7 Trinity Street). It was presumably built earlier in the 17th Century before the development of Newtown; it was supposedly in the ownership of the Castle family for a while (hence the street name, which like many others in this area uses the name of the principal resident for its own purpose - William Gentle, the Naishs, the Buttons, the Hortons, and so on are other such examples), but who planted on the brick façade, possibly the first such in Frome? It seems to be 18th Century work, rather than, as could be possible, of 1875[24].

In 1897 another building which was later to form part of the hospital provision in Frome was erected for the Church of England Society, in what was then open countryside in Green Lane. This was known as the "St Aldhelm's Home", and it had accommodation for up to 48 orphaned boys, and trained them for various trades. Included on the site was a small printing workshop, which must have guaranteed employment for many of the boys as the firm of Butler and Tanner had by then developed into being Frome's largest employer. It survived in this usage until some time after 1950, when it was converted into a geriatric hospital. It had a major reshaping and extension in 1984/85, and as a result of a public subscription which raised some £30,000 a new day room was constructed, to replace the former dayroom converted from the old printing workshop, also through the proceeds of a public appeal, about 1970. The building was closed down just before it was due to celebrate its centenary, as new accommodation (The Chantry Buildings) had been then provided behind the Victoria Hospital; it has been converted into apartments.

As part of the celebrations of Queen Victoria's Diamond Jubilee in 1897 an appeal was launched to provide Frome with a new purpose-built hospital, at an estimated cost of £3,500, of which the Revd W. A. Duckworth of Orchardleigh contributed £1,000. The architect was Bertie V. Johnson, one of Duckworth's relatives, who also designed Westbury Hospital: these buildings must have been carried out at the beginning of his career, as Johnson became President of the Royal Institute of British Architects in 1940[25]. The grounds were laid out by Alfred Parsons, R.A., who lived in Frome. The building, which opened as the Victoria Hospital in 1901, was later extended at the front, where the

42

outpatients' department is located, and at the rear, where nurses' accommodation was provided in the 1930s. A physiotherapy unit was established north of the main hospital in 1980, again thanks to a public subscription which raised £40,000, representing half of the total cost. Yet again, in 1999/2000, the public of Frome were faced with a further public appeal, this time towards the building of a new hospital on part of the former Frome Show site off Bath Road - the fate of the present buildings is currently uncertain, although there is a current proposal to convert them into a Steiner school.

To continue the story of medical provision in the town, although it again breaks the chronological sequence: prior to 1969 Frome's medical practices were based in several places, with the principal practice accommodated in West Lodge, Christchurch Street West, (firstly in the single storey building closest to the road, where signs of the old steps up to the doorway can still be seen in the wall, and then on the south side of the building in a flat-roofed extension which was entered from Weymouth Road). This house has been occupied almost since it was built by members of the medical profession, although the present owner is now retired. In 1969 the County Council designed and erected a new Health Centre on land adjacent to the hospital in Park Road, and all of the local practices merged and moved to the centre, which could provide more facilities than the individual practices ever could. This centre has developed since then, and major enlargements made in the middle 1990s meant that even more professionals could be accommodated: in addition a local chemist relocated from Badcox to the site so that the centre can be even better used.

There was another important development in the town in 1875: the merging of all the various markets in the town (which included the covered market in the Market Place, and also those markets previously held in Trinity Street), and the construction of the Market Hall (now known as the Cheese & Grain Building). This was another relatively early brick building in the town, by Frome standards. It must have brought considerable prosperity to the town, because it afforded excellent facilities not only for the display and marketing of goods, especially local cheese, but by dint of a lift, storage facilities and a railway siding at the rear (onto what is now used only as a mineral railway line from Hapsford Quarry), it meant that goods could be brought into the town, sold and easily transported away again as necessary. Not only was this a boost for local commerce, but the hall was used for meetings and social gatherings, as well as, from 1905, the earliest performances of the Frome Amateur Operatic Society. Naturally it was the focal point of the annual Frome Cheese Show, which was held in the field now occupied by the Market Yard car park[26]. (Sundry buildings were added over the years to accommodate the twice-weekly agricultural market, but eventually this outgrew the facilities available - and the chaos of cattle transporters manoeuvring in the Market Yard every Wednesday will not easily be forgotten by those who experienced them - and with the aid of a considerable grant from the European Community a new agricultural market was built three miles away at Standerwick in the late 1980s.) Meanwhile, the Market Hall, which had been used by Messrs Singers for the production of shell cases during the First World War, had ceased being used for its original function, and became part of a furniture factory, and later a retail outlet. Eventually left empty, the property was taken over by the Mendip District Council, who demolished the ancillary accommodation and revamped the area; the hall was then passed

43

on to the Frome Town Council, who adapted it for public use again and reopened it as The Cheese and Grain Building in 1998.

Another small hall used for public assemblies was built in High Street in 1880; originally a Gospel Hall, it was used by the Young Men's Christian Association for many years before it became the Frome Labour Hall; the Frome Working Men's Club, founded in 1882, also had its roots there[27]. It was later used by the Frome branch of The Ancient Order of Buffaloes.

In 1891 the Frome Board of Guardians, who had been formed in 1834 to take over the civil parish administration, and their next-door neighbours the Poor Law Union, who had been located in Nos 16/17 Bath Street, decided that their 18th Century premises were no longer adequate, and so they erected new Public Offices in Christchurch Street West, next door to Christ Church, on the site of an old smithy. This building was designed by Anderson and Halliday, and erected by Joseph Bird, a Radstock builder, using stone quarried from The Butts (which would have been either from the old Seward's yard - now the site of the new housing development known as Newington Close - or further down where Richmond Road is now located), with Bath stone dressings[28]. The Board was to enjoy it for only 3 years before they were replaced by the Frome Urban District Council, who shared the building with the newly formed Frome Rural District Council. During the 1930s the U.D.C found it necessary to expand into Oriel Cottage, across the road (now a sewing materials shop and beauty parlour), and they left completely in 1955 when they purchased North Hill House which they then adapted as their offices. Upon the local government reorganisation in 1974 the Public Offices were passed over to the new Mendip District Council, who leased it to the Somerset County Council apart from the one room used for a time by the newly formed Frome Town Council. The building is now used as the area headquarters of the County Council Social Services, not so very different from the Poor Law union of a century or so ago. (After serving as a regional office for the Mendip District Council until their headquarters building in Shepton Mallet had been completed, North Hill House became commercial offices before its present use as a private school.)

The Diamond Jubilee of Queen Victoria's reign was celebrated in a great wave of patriotic fervour in Frome, with the provision not only of the hospital but other public facilities for the town. The Golden Jubilee in 1887 had seen the purchase of land to form the Victoria Park, for the general recreation of the townspeople in what was for a short while the countryside outside Frome (although by 1897 the old track known as Somerset Lane had become Somerset Road as houses were built to overlook the new park both here and in Weymouth Road). Another recreational facility was built - the Victoria (public) Baths - just off Bath Street in what is nowadays known as Rook Lane. In this case the building was not entirely new, but a conversion of a former foundry belonging to Cockey's Ironworks (of which more later). Frome was apparently one of the first towns (outside the City of Westminster) to be able to boast of such a facility. The architect for the conversion was H Moore. The building included slipper baths as well as a swimming pool, and continued in use until 1975, after the new pool at the Frome Sports Centre complex at Frome College had been opened[29]. After reverting back to industrial premises for a short

44

while, the building was demolished to provide additional car parking for the area, and subsequently new housing.

There is one 19th Century building which I was unable to date until I saw an old photograph of it, displaying a datestone of 1828, and that is the old Fire Engine House in Christchurch Street West, in the north-west corner of Christ Church churchyard. (Its siting was not unusual in days when the civil and religious parishes were the same thing - the blindhouse was a similar "churchyard facility".) This was a more sensible place to keep it than in St Andrew's Chapel in St John's Church, its original accommodation, or in its subsequent location of the undercroft to Church House at the bottom of Church Steps, because unless there was a horse available the engine had to be dragged manually to the fire, and it was rather better downhill than up - and most of the newer development in the 19th Century was "Behind Town" along Portway, The Butts and Keyford! The building was probably enlarged or rebuilt more than once, and it remained the garage for Frome's fire engines until 1970, when the County Council built the new fire station on the site of the former Unicorn Inn at the junction of Keyford and the Butts, a good strategic site from which to serve the town. The old building still survives: the two front door arches were turned into one, and the building converted into offices[30].

After the burst of building activity around 1900, there was a short lull before the next public building, the Post Office, was opened in the Market Place, having previously been located first in Vicarage Street and then at No 6 Bath Street. This was not a completely new building, but was converted out of the old Bull's Temperance Hotel. It would seem that the public area changed little since then - sometimes to the chagrin of Frome residents - but the sorting office was relocated to Vallis Way in the mid 1990s, and the post office finally closed its doors in 2004 (supposedly on commercial grounds), with the business being transferred to Messrs Martins in the Westway Precinct.

In 1913 the Co-operative Society started building works in Palmer Street, and included in their project was their coal order office (now used as a private day nursery) and a meeting hall over it. This was used for a wide range of events, and for some years in the 1970s and 1980s served first as a bingo hall and then as the headquarters of the Frome Amateur Operatic Society, before they took on the responsibilities of running the Frome Memorial Hall (q.v.). Despite the (now badly decayed) datestone of 1913, the hall was opened on April 4th of the following year. The buildings were erected by a Mr Parsons to the design of a Mr Harris[31]. The hall and the other former Co-op buildings in Palmer Street/ Bath Street, added to the design of Percy Rigg in 1923, were converted into business premises which will include a restaurant and night club.

With unforeseen good timing, the new Keyford Territorial Army Drill Hall opened on St Valentine's Day 1914 - another of the relatively few brick buildings in the central area of the town, and presumably not the work of a local designer[32]. For many years the Drill Hall had been in Gentle Street, along the south wall of St John's churchyard, and it subsequently, in conjunction with No 1 Gentle Street, became the United Services Club: when that folded in the 1970s it became an Old Peoples' Day Centre for some 15 years, but eventually this too closed down.

The First World War put an end to all building works, apart from those necessarily part of the war effort, but things slowly picked up after the Armistice in 1918. An appeal was launched in Frome to provide a fitting memorial to the town's War Dead, with the intention of erecting a new Assembly Hall. The old home of the Cockey family, South Hill House in Christchurch Street West, was purchased and demolished, and Percy Rigg, the Frome architect who had an office in the undercroft to Monmouth House, was commissioned to design the building. The presentation drawing for this still survives (in the ownership of Nugent Vallis Brierley, the successors - via Ronald Vallis and his son Bill - to Percy Rigg's practice), and is quite impressive; sadly, Frome could not raise enough money to build it, and a very much cheaper scheme had to be substituted to enable the work to be started in 1923. The fact that Percy Rigg was also the business manager for the Frome Amateur Operatic Society for many years was probably one reason for this Society using this building for every one of their productions since 1925. However, apart from usage by the Frome British Legion once a year (there are War Memorials in the foyer) the hall was not a commercial success, and by 1931 it was leased out by the Trustees to become a "talking picture theatre", and so the "Grand Cinema" as it was then christened remained in use as such until 1985. It is now in permanent use as a theatre, manned by volunteers (mostly members of the Operatic Society), who have made considerable improvements to the building, notably to the formerly very stark façade, over the last few years.

Originally there was only one rival to this cinema, the "Palace Theatre" on Church Steps, formerly the Mechanics' Institute. It was smaller and inferior, and did not last long once the Gaumont Cinema (on the site of the present-day Westway Cinema in Cork Street) opened its doors in the mid 1930s. This was to last for about 40 years before the whole area was redeveloped commercially in the early 1970s. Things might have been even more competitive had the "Vaudeville Pavilion" (located in Christchurch Street East) made a go of things: it opened to packed houses on September 18th 1922, but by November 9th of that year it had been closed down by the magistrates as being unfit, and a danger to the public, and never reopened!

No-one could claim that the Frome Memorial Hall, as it is now properly known, was ideal for use as a theatre, despite many attempts to refurbish it, but it was not until the 1970s that Frome had a purpose-built theatre. This, the Merlin Theatre, is part of the Frome Community College complex, and is the result of a partnership between the Somerset County Council, as the education authority, and a private trust, resulting in a drama teaching space for the College when it is in session, and a public theatre at other times. It was opened in 1974, and in recent years has become the central focus for media studies, which are now an important and acclaimed part of the courses on offer at Frome College. A similar arrangement was used for the Sports Centre next door, but here the second partner is Mendip District Council, as successor to the Frome UDC and Frome RDC which were in office when the scheme was set up. In its time a somewhat pioneering development; it has been a means of ensuring that Frome does have reasonable facilities for sport and recreation for a town of its size.

The 1960s and 1970s saw a new wave of building in Frome, and saw the construction of, amongst the public buildings, Northover House, in North Parade, used as government offices, (probably designed by the Ministry of Public Building and Works, as it was then), and the Public Library in Scott Road (now the shop premises of Ellenbray Press) designed by Vallis and Vallis. Both were of the late 1960s, and it has to be said that neither was really suitable for the prominent sites that they occupied in what has since been declared as the central Conservation Area. The former was demolished in 2004 to make way for houses; the latter soon proved too small for the developing requirements of the town, and another new library, designed by the County Council Architects' Department, was opened about 1990 in the corner of the Market Yard: whilst not beautiful, it is more appropriate to its surroundings. It also related well to the town's Tourist Information Centre, which was located in a former drying tower of the dye works in Justice Lane, and to the current home of the Frome Museum.

Just as this survey of Frome's public buildings has revealed a little of the social history of the town, so will reviews of its industrial and commercial buildings, and these will be the subject of the next two chapters.

FOOTNOTES

1   Michael McGarvie: "The Book of Frome": Barracuda Books, 1980; and also his "Frome Through The Ages": Frome Society for Local Study, 1982.

2.   Michael McGarvie: Op. cit.

3.   Samuel Cuzner: "Cuzner's Handbook to Froome Selwood": Cuzner, 1866; published to commemorate both the completion of the restoration of St John's Church and an "Art and Industrial Exhibition" held in Frome in that year.

4.   Peter Belham: "The Blue House Restored": (an article therein): Blue House Appeal Committee, 1965.

5.   Samuel Cuzner: Op. cit.

6.   Peter Belham: "The Making of Frome": Frome Society for Local Study, 1973.

7.   Francis Kelly: (investigator for) The Department for the Environment's Statutory List of Buildings of Special Architectural or Historic Interest- Frome, Somerset: 1983. (This list, summarised at the end of this book in the Appendix, also contains short descriptions of each feature or building listed, although they were intended only to facilitate the identity of the Listed item).

8.   Peter Belham: Op. cit.

9.   Derek Gill: "Experiences of a 19th Century Gentleman" (edited version of Thomas Bunn's Diaries): Frome Society for Local Study, 2003.

10. Michael McGarvie: Op. cit.

11. Michael McGarvie: Op. cit.

12. Michael McGarvie: Op. cit.

13. Derek Gill: "Frome School Days": Frome 1300 Publications, 1985.

14. Michael McGarvie: Op. cit.

15. Rodney Goodall: "Eighty Years of Frome": (an article therein): booklet published by the Frome Urban District Council on its demise in 1974.

16. Derek Gill: "The Story of Christ Church, Frome" BPC, 1974.

17. Harvey and others: "The Frome Almanack": various (yearly) volumes.

18. Michael McGarvie: Op. cit.

19. Peter Belham: Op. cit.

20. Michael McGarvie: "Frome in Old Picture Postcards" Volume 2: European Library, 1984.

21. Harvey and others: "The Frome Almanack": various (yearly) volumes.

22. Peter Belham: Op. cit.

23. Michael McGarvie: "Frome in Old Picture Postcards" volume 2: European Library, 1984.

24. Roger Leach and Derek Gill: "Early Industrial Housing - The Trinity Area of Frome": Royal Commission on Historic Monuments Supplementary Series No. 3: HMSO, 1981.

25. Journal of the Royal Institute of British Architects, 150th Anniversary Issue, 1984.

26. Anon: "A History of Frome Cheese Show 1877-1977": Frome and District Agricultural Society, 1977.

27. Derek Gill: "The Sheppards and Eighteenth Century Frome": Frome Society for Local Study, 1982.

28. H Balch: "Eighty Years of Frome": (an article therein): Frome Urban District Council, 1974.

29. Michael McGarvie: Op. cit.

30. Peter Belham: Op. cit.

31. Harvey and others: "The Frome Almanack": various (yearly) volumes

32. Harvey and others: Op. cit.

## CHRIST CHURCH OLD SCHOOL, PARK ROAD

Designed for the Revd. Richard Meade in 1844 by Sir George Gilbert Scott, later extended, and now converted into eight flats.

## FROME RAILWAY STATION

The original broad gauge station, designed by Brunel's assistant T R Hannaford, and opened in 1850, little changed over the years. (A R Yeates)

## FORMER DYE-HOUSE IN JUSTICE LANE

As it was before restoration.
(G F J Russell)

## FORMER DYE-HOUSE IN JUSTICE LANE

Now restored and previously the Town Information Centre.
( A R Yeates)

# CHAPTER SIX

# THE INDUSTRIAL BUILDINGS OF FROME

The story of Frome's industry (which I have related in more detail elsewhere)[1] is dominated by that of the woollen industry, which was the principal business in the town for much of its history. A number of the sites of the old woollen mills are clearly identifiable, but few of their buildings now survive. Of the Sheppards' mills (the Sheppards being the major woollen cloth firm in Frome from the middle of the 17th Century until 1878) little survives: their works at Spring Gardens, where most of their production was centred, deteriorated quickly after they closed down, and after a serious fire about 1900 they were demolished[2]. Of their earlier premises in the centre of Frome, at the Town Mill, (on the river bank opposite Willow Vale, and behind the Blue House[3]) the last wall was demolished in the early 1970s, but in Willow Vale itself one or two outbuildings survive from their complex of buildings (they were linked to the other river bank by a footbridge, which was washed away in floods in 1932 killing some boys who were on it at the time, so it was never replaced[4]. The site of the bridge is marked by a gate in the railings in Willow Vale). The Mansard roofed warehouse behind Nos 5 and 5 A, of about 1820, and possibly a garage-like building further down Willow Vale, may be survivors from the Sheppards' establishment. The dye tower in the garden of one of the houses in Willow Vale is another relic of the Sheppards: they used, if not owned, a major dyeing house here which had twelve vats and seven furnaces for the drying of the cloth after dyeing. (The main surviving legacy of the Sheppards consists of some of their grand houses, including Iron Gates, Court House and Fromefield House, as well as the old school building opposite this last.)

At the risk of ignoring the chronology of the other woollen mills in the town and its immediate surroundings, it would seem sensible to take the mills in sequence along the River Frome, starting first with the tributary Rodden Brook[5]. Rodden Mill was owned by the Sheppards, but has gone completely. Another outlier was the West Woodlands Mill, (1794-1883), which has also long since been demolished. Feltham Mill was in existence by 1827 as a fulling mill, but little else is recorded. The Friggle Street Mill dated from at least 1616, and was described as a tucking mill; it was refurbished in 1798, and demolished by 1885. Back on the River Frome, the St John's Mill, at Adderwell, is not well recorded: it was used for a while by the firm of Houston & Son, later becoming a rubber factory: the last vestiges of the mill were demolished in 1964, the site being partly occupied by Messrs Butler and Tanner and partly by Messrs Cuprinol (who closed their operation in Frome at the beginning of the 21st Century).

Wallbridge had two mills: the first, the Wallbridge Mill, existed by 1727, and was used for many years for grinding animal feedstuffs, finally closing in the 1980s: it has now been converted into a private house. The Wallbridge Factory, on the other side of the Warminster Road, was initially (in the early 18th Century) a dye-house, run by the Meares family of Corsley; after it was sold in 1834 it became a woollen mill: it was rebuilt by Alfred Tucker in 1868, after he bought the business, and his firm continued producing Tucker's West of England tweed there until 1965[6]. The premises were then adapted for carpet manufacture, being used successively by Marley, Venture Carpets and Coloroll; when the last named went under in the 1990s the factory closed. Some buildings on the south side of the road were adapted into small industrial units, but most of the buildings on the north side were demolished in 2000/ 2001 to make way for housing.

Continuing along the river, the Town Mill (Sheppards') has already been mentioned; then came Welsh Mill: this was used for fulling, weaving and dyeing by the Jesser family in the mid-18th Century, but by 1810 it was being leased by Thomas Napper, who built a new factory adjoining the mill. The mill was later taken over by Houston & Son and continued in use until the early 20th Century: it was demolished some time before the river was diverted through the site around 1970 as a flood prevention measure. Next came Leonard's Mill: this existed by 1700 when it was run by Robert Smith (builder of both Rook Lane House in Christchurch Street West, and the Rook Lane Chapel, in part of what was his garden[7]). It was extended by tenants John Grant and James Slade in 1818. The mill was sold in 1828, and was converted to a corn mill in 1840. Most of the buildings have long since gone, but part of the original fulling mill may have been adapted as one of the buildings of the Frome sewage works, now occupying the site. There was also a mill at Egford, on the Mells Brook, which was one of the establishments run by Harry Hams, and further along the same stream was Hapsford Mill, near Great Elm, founded by George George about 1785, which by 1830 was said to employ 600 people (many of whom were probably outworkers, who may have worked for other clothiers as well). Some buildings from the latter may in part survive at Hapsford: the factory transferred to Staplemead Mill, Old Ford, in 1859[8] (to the site occupied by Express Dairies, then Arla, but it is not thought that any of that mill survives).

At Spring Gardens there were two other establishments apart from the Sheppards' mill: there was a small mill owned by the Champneys of Orchardleigh, which may survive in part, and Jefferies Mill[9], which dates from about 1804, and which contained a fullers' and dressers' factory until about 1900: it is now converted into two houses. A little further along the river was White Mill, also owned by the Champneys: it existed by 1727, and was used by Houston & Son until the end of the 19th Century, when it was demolished. Further still came Beckington and Shawford Mills, but these were not presumably worked by Frome people, and are outside the scope of this book.

As mechanisation gradually crept in (with much spirited opposition from some of the woollen workers, who smashed machinery in several of the adjacent towns and even set fire to some mills away from Frome) other establishments were set up away from the river, making use of the newly introduced steam power instead of running water. Amongst these was a mill in The Butts occupied by Edward Napper by 1813, (and later by the Hams family, who also had a mill at Egford and another factory in South Parade), but this has disappeared and the site has not been identified. Another factory was built in 1807 in South Parade for Samuel Humphreys, but this was burnt down (probably by arson) in 1821 and not rebuilt; some of the outbuildings were absorbed into a carding factory (q.v.). A mill in Broadway is mentioned by 1825, having various occupants including Houston & Son, and it survived until 1904, when, after failing to sell as a going concern, the mill was demolished to make way for houses. Nearby, in Vallis Way, the Brittain family built a factory in 1823, part of which was let out to other clothiers. A partner in the concern, Henry Houston, took over soon after 1833, and the factory was rebuilt in 1866: the business continued until 1924, when it was merged with Carrs of Twerton; the premises were demolished in 1964 to enable the Wallington & Weston site to be expanded[10]. As well as steam power, one Frome factory used horse power (literally) and was said to be making 12 to 15 pieces of cloth (presumably per week); its site has not been identified.

The Jesser family had been clothiers and dyers in Welshmill for many years, and one of the family, Thomas Jesser, also made high quality carpets, winning a prize for one of his works: it was his daughter who built Argyll House in Gentle Street. Another factory, producing silk and crepe, was opened by William Thompson (later joined by Philip Le Gros, of North Hill House) in 1823, in Merchant's Barton, (this employed some 400 people by the end of the 19th Century, and there was another factory at Shepton Mallet) and this continued in production until about 1926: the premises were taken over by two other businesses, Notts Industries and Beswicks Alert Fuse Works. The former is still in operation on the site, using some of the old mill buildings; the latter (having been taken over by Cooper Bussman) announced at the end of 2000 that it was transferring production to the Far East and closing the Frome factory: the future of these buildings is subject to the development of Saxonvale and Garsdale.

The woollen industry needed various supporting industries, and some of these were to be found in Frome. The dyeing industry was strong in the area, but few significant fragments remain; perhaps the most evident is the drying tower in Justice Lane, which was part of the dyeworks run by the Olive Family. A number of families of dyers existed in the area, including the Parishes of Shawford, the Buttons of Welshmill, the Allens of Low Water (whose dyeworks is perpetuated in the name Dyers' Close Lane), the Backhouses of Rodden Lake, the Meares of Wallbridge and, of course, the Olives of both Frome and Shawford. Dyeing was initially confined to blue cloth, using the woad plant which grew locally. The "Oad Grounds" where this was grown became the site of the Newtown, or Trinity Area, in due course: the Rack Fields, where the cloth was set out to dry, were where the Memorial Theatre now stands. Other colours used were brown (from yew), red (from hedge bedstraw) and purple (from lichens treated with urine). Later, artificial dyestuffs were made in the town by James Holroyd, who had buildings near Frome Railway Station, parts of which remain[11].

Another supporting industry was carding - the manufacture of wire-toothed combs (similar to those used to groom pets today) which supplanted the locally grown teasels (which were unpleasant to handle, and of which a constant supply could not be guaranteed) before 1700. Frome was a major centre for their manufacture, and by 1738 the Frome Carders had their own trade association. In 1800 there were 20 carding firms in the town, but these gradually dwindled to two. The larger, Samuel Rawlings and Son (or S & T Rawlings, as it became) had been established as a family concern some time in the 17th Century, and they survived in Frome, on the corner of South Parade and Christchurch Street West, until 1972, when the Yorkshire firm who had taken them over some years previously relocated to Yorkshire[12]. Their premises survive almost intact (they mostly date from the 19th Century, one of the main buildings having a datestone - now eroded - of 1831), and have been converted to flats. (I visited the factory in 1971, and it must surely have been the last in Frome where the clerks still sat at desks which ran all round the walls, on high stools, made laborious entries in ledgers by hand: had there been funding and sufficient interest this would have made an excellent industrial museum!). The other survivor was George Hinchcliffe, in Christchurch Street East, who lasted until the end of the 19th Century[13].

There were many small clothiers in Frome throughout the years, many of whom would rent premises in the main mills as necessary, and who probably shared some of the out-workers as well - but all are gone without trace. There were also uses for the waste products of the cloth-making: a good example was the hat-making firm of William Portman & Co who were located near the railway station: they used the trimmings from the cloth to make felt for their hats. Another hat maker was John Nicholls, who had an establishment in the Market Place (and at 2 Bath Street). Once mechanisation reached the industry, there was a need for engineers to make and maintain the machinery. Two local firms, Rogers and Fishers, made steam engines, and Abraham Haley, of Selwood Iron Works in The Butts (on the site of, and behind, the former Amoco Garage), as a millwright and general engineer, specialised in making looms (Webbs of Trowbridge, who sold out in 1896, had a complete set of Haley looms); later, the firm branched out into motor car manufacture, and the Albion car was made here. Part of these works still survived, behind the new buildings.

But now we have reached engineering, it is time to follow the history of another major industry in Frome - that of metal foundry. The beginnings were small: about 1684 William Cockey set up a small bell foundry in Bell Lane, which was part of the Trinity Area (he lived in Whittox Lane) and until 1752 they cast church bells here (the business of bell founding carried on until about 1850, but had relocated). One bell was made for St John's Church in Frome, two were made for Farleigh Hungerford, and many others bearing the Cockey name may be found in the region - however, it is said that their tone was not of the best, and most have been recast! Nevertheless, the family name continued in Frome, and by 1814 another branch of the family was developing a cast iron foundry under the direction of Edward Cockey, whose family had lived at 15 Bath Street since 1773. Presumably working from home, the business grew up behind the house (later extending sideways and rearwards until there were entrances to the foundry from Bath Street and Palmer Street. Little remains of their first premises, apart from a cast iron hoist on the face of their building in Palmer Street. The firm cast all kinds of components, especially street furniture (many drain gratings, guardrails, lamp posts, etc. in Frome still carry the Cockey name, and some of their electric light standards, specially made for Frome when mains electricity was introduced into the town in 1903, are now "Listed" and protected); but perhaps their biggest venture was into making components for the newly emerging gas industry. To help promote their business, Edward Cockey set up the Frome Gas Company in 1831 (with himself as the company secretary, of course)[14]. The first building to be lit by gas was Mr Penny's shop and printing press at 7 Bath Street, almost opposite their premises. The first gasometer (which they made, inevitably) was in the Market Yard: in 1884 they built a more sophisticated gasworks alongside the branch railway at Welshmill. (The latter premises have been demolished: the Frome Gas Company merged with that of

Bath in 1934). After the advent of the railway in 1850, Cockeys began to relocate to Wallbridge, where they built a substantial foundry which included their own rail sidings, enabling the easy transport of their products, which later included steam engines and building components, all over the country. At one time they are said to have employed 800 people, and their goods were exported as far as Russia. Some of their buildings remained, one still bearing the company name on the gable, although the firm finally closed in 1960, and the premises were taken over by ARC (now Hansons, as a vehicle depot) and Matbro, machinery manufacturers. They have now been demolished to make way for housing.

Another major engineering firm, still going strong in the town, is Messrs J W Singer. Strangely, they could be said to owe their existence to the Church, and particularly the Tractarian Movement, brought to Frome by Vicar Bennett (who had arrived in Frome in 1852). Joseph Singer was born in Frome in 1819, and educated at the Blue School. He trained as a watchmaker in London, later returning to Frome to manage a local shop. About 1854, having made a pair of brass candlesticks for a local church, he was encouraged by Vicar Bennett to set up business on his own, making brass candleholders, vases, crucifixes and such ecclesiastical items, gradually expanding into larger items such as brass lecterns and screens (there is a fine screen by him in St John's Church)[15]. His reputation spread, and he was soon making artefacts for the Oxford colleges. He opened a shop in Frome Market Place (next door to what is now Lloyds TSB Bank), and later opened a London shop as well. His first small forge was in Eagle Lane, behind his shop: later he bought a house at Waterloo (West End), and the factory developed in his garden, his house later becoming the offices (when he moved to Knoll House, in Bath Street). The twelve hands employed in 1866 soon became 200 or so. They moved on to bronze casting, specialising in statuary: many famous London statues are their castings, including the figure of Justice on The Old Bailey, and Queen Boadicea on the Thames Embankment opposite the Houses of Parliament. (The horses which form part of the latter were carried around in the town's procession commemorating Queen Victoria's Diamond Jubilee)[16]. Having been requisitioned in the First World War to make shell cases, they returned to statuary immediately afterwards, casting many of the war memorials around the country (legend has it that the one which now stands outside their new factory in Wessex Fields was one that was "left over"). In 1914 they had merged with Messrs Spital & Clark of London, and gradually their principal work changed to the hot brass pressings, especially for the plumbing and allied trades, which are their main product today. They moved to their new site in 1999, and in the following year their old premises were demolished to make way for new houses.

Another significant industry in Frome is that of printing. The earliest recorded printer seems to have been Abraham Crocker, a master at the Blue School, who set up a part- time press at the Blue House in 1795, which his elder son John carried on in conjunction with a bookshop and library, which was established in the then newly-built 7 Bath Street by 1815. Crocker's second son, James, ran a similar business in Cheap Street, but died in 1820, when his widow sold the business to William Ponsford Penny. When John died in 1831, Penny bought this business as well, so merging the Crocker interests. Penny's firm survived for the rest of the 19th Century, being run by his widow and two sons after he died in 1851; the business was sold by a grandson in 1905 to W G White. They had specialised in printing church books, magazines and so on, and even ran a local newspaper, The Frome Times, forerunner of The Somerset Standard. In 1915 White sold the shop, which then became a branch of W H Smith, who at that time carried on a similar business, and they remained there until 1972. (Ironically, after a gap of some 30 years or so, Messrs W H Smith returned to Frome, to part of the former Halford's premises, in 2002.) Another press which developed in Frome was the Ellenbray Press, which was started by Charles Bray in the early 20th Century, some time before 1915. (It was named after his daughter, who lived to be 102 years old, dying in 1983, and who was one of Frome's great characters.) Their press, originally in The Old Vicarage House, King Street, moved to Christchurch Street West (next to the Memorial Theatre), and later was taken over by the Dowland Press, which has since closed.

However, Frome's largest printers (indeed, they were still said to be the largest privately-owned printing press in Europe) is Messrs Butler and Tanner. They had small beginnings: in 1844 William Thomas Butler joined William Langford, the chemist at 20 Bath Street as a partner, and in the following year as business prospered they started a small press in a former stable in the yard of the nearby Wheatsheaf Inn to print the labels and leaflets for their patent medicines, employing a manager to carry out the work. By 1854 they had parted company, and Butler had removed to Castle House, Castle Street, where he continued printing. He accumulated so much outside business that he set up a steam press in 1857. Butler took on Joseph Tanner as a partner in this new venture, but retired in 1867, leaving the firm in the hands of the Tanner family[17]. As it turned out, the choice of the Trinity Area for such a venture was inspired: the leases on some of the houses were due to expire again, meaning there was possible room for expansion; and as the woollen industry collapsed, many of the workers formerly employed by the mills who lived in this area found work at the rapidly expanding press. Gradually adjoining houses were purchased and demolished, and in 1866, when they were employing over 150 people, construction began of their Selwood Printing Works, designed by Joseph Chapman jr the stonemason: it was erected in instalments, the last extension being in 1911. By 1892 their rival White, in a Frome guidebook, stated that their 1889 production amounted to 12 million books, magazines and pamphlets. However, they began to run out of space, and in 1908 had begun the transfer to their present site at Adderwell, using part of the site of the old St John's Mill. The old premises continued in use, latterly as storage for printed books for the London publishers, until they were condemned by the Health and Safety Inspectorate; they have now been converted into flats, as the premises were Listed, being deemed worthy of preservation as part of Frome's history. Their Adderwell works expanded over part of the old railway sidings, and now their computerised machinery is some of the most modem in the world. Butler and Tanner did not survive, but were saved by Felix Dennis and have subsequently traded as Butler, Tanner and Dennis.

Another major industry in the town was brewing - it is said that the very hard Frome water was ideal for the bitter varieties of beer. Of course, beer was originally made by the individual public houses, but it was more efficient when houses combined in a joint brewery (although the last few years have seen a revival in small pub-based breweries, amongst which can be counted the Griffin Inn in Milk Street). One of the earlier breweries in the town was the Badcox Brewery, run by the Trotman family from 1820; it later became part of the Frome United Breweries. Their premises, originally a cloth mill, were demolished in 1959 to make way for the council houses of Vallis Way, Broadway and Dorset Close. Close by was the Swan Brewery at Badcox, adjacent to the Swan Inn, which stood where the car par at Badcox is now; this was run by the Baily family, who were very prominent in the area in the brewing industry, running public houses (including The Bath Arms, Palmer Street; The Bell Inn, Trinity Street; the Lamb Inn at Gorehedge, and Mansford & Baily - The Wheatsheaf- in Bath Street), breweries, malthouses, etc in East Somerset and much of Wiltshire. This family also ran the Lamb Brewery at Gorehedge (which occupied the whole of the triangular site of the present road junction as well as some premises on the north side of Christchurch Street East - with some buildings converted into the flats known as The Maltings): this was demolished between 1959 and 1961. This brewery had been designed in 1858 by James Oxley, a Frome brewery engineer (of whom more below) "adopting the best practices of Burton on Trent" (then the country's most prominent brewing town). The output of this brewery was prodigious, and took up the supplies from four malthouses, including their own in Gentle Street. The Baily family ran a large maltings down by the railway station, now almost totally demolished after it closed around 1960. Another maltings was located in Willow Vale; parts were demolished to make way for the Masonic Hall in North Parade, but some buildings survive, much altered. Yet other maltings existed in Locks Hill and Whittox Lane. Brewing of a slightly different kind was carried out at Welshmill by the Frome Vinegar Brewing Company: some of their premises were adapted to form offices, in what is now the west end of Park Hill Drive.

To support the brewing industry there was an important local firm of brewery engineers, originally trading in the mid 19th Century as Oxley and Geoghegan; later they became Wilson & Co, and finally Wilson and Scotchman. They were originally located at Welshmill, but moved to Keyford about 1900, having also run a cooperage in The Butts until then. They were said to be one of the biggest firms of their kind in the country, and they made vats, mashing machines, pumps, coppers, steam engines, coolers, and so on, and their 150 employees included sawyers, coppersmiths, and foundrymen. Messrs Guiness of Dublin were said to be their best customer. Of their premises, very little now survives: the Welshmill site was occupied by housing, the site at The Butts became a builder's yard which eventually gave way for housing in 1999, and the site at Keyford, which survived until the last Mr Scotchman died in the 1970s, was eventually cleared to make way for the housing estate now known as The Cooperage.

The building industry is obviously important in any consideration of the buildings of Frome, and yet not much is recorded of Frome's builders before the 20th Century, and although their projects are still here for us to see, their yards and premises have mostly disappeared. One of the first recorded builders is James Pope, who may also have been an amateur designer of some note: he was credited as being the builder of Rook Lane Chapel, and also of the tower of the Church of West Woodlands. In the 19th Century, William Brown seems to have been the major builder in the town; by 1837 he was busy converting the premises at 16/17 Bath Street for the Frome Board of Guardians (forerunners of the

Frome Town Council), and Frederick and George Brown (his children) were responsible for the virtual rebuilding of St John's Church between 1860 and 1866. Cuzner speaks of Frederick and George Brown as "having been established between 50 and 60 years" (in other words, about 1810). "Their works are among the largest in the county of Somerset, and are situated at Pilly Vale (Willow Vale) and King Street, Froome".

William George Brown is credited as a designer at Christ Church in 1868 who, as architect, extended this church between 1899 and 1905, and who designed and lived in St Martins, Park Road. However, the building works at Christ Church were carried out by Barnes the Builders, suggesting that Browns may have ceased to exist by this time. It seems that the stonemasons Joseph Chapman, father and son, were very active as builders in the town: the father had built the screen to St John's Church forecourt, and a new west front to the church itself (removed c 1860) in 1815. Cuzner says the firm was founded about 1805, and exported carved marble and stone to many of the countries of the British Empire, even as far as New Zealand. The son was also active as an architect and monumental stonemason, and designed (and possibly built?) the Selwood Printing Works in the Trinity Area, and reshaped Zion Church in Whittox Lane in 1888. He also designed (but did not build, the builder being Thomas Parfitt) the Temperance Hall in Catherine Street in 1874/75, and his own very eccentric house at 44 Portway, which dates from 1867. He designed the chapel at the Dissenters' cemetery.

Another major builder was F J Seward, founded in 1873. They took over the old cooperage buildings of Wilson & Scotchman in The Butts in 1900, and remained in business working from there until 1966. They built a number of the streets of houses in Frome, including Weymouth Road, Somerset Road and probably some of The Butts; they ran their own quarry at Old Ford, and worked on some of the local churches; and in the 1930s they rebuilt Mells Manor to the design of Sir Edwin Lutyens after the earlier building had been destroyed by fire. Their yard became a builder's merchants, but closed in 1998, and the area was cleared for more housing - a fate which befell the yard of another local builder, Hodders, who were based in Nunney Road, and who had built many of the houses in that area. A local firm which developed much of the post-war housing in Frome was the firm of Williams Brothers, who constructed parts of Oakfield Road, including St Aldhelm's Close, Charles Road and Foster Road, and the Berkley Down Estate: they were located at the top of Wesley Close, off Christchurch Street West, and their offices and workshops (formerly an ironworks according to the 1886 O S map) are now occupied by Messrs Hornbeam Ivy and Nunney Road Garage.

Despite being a general industrial town by the end of the 19th Century, Frome still had some businesses which indicated its agricultural roots, one of which was the tanning of leather. Tanning is first recorded at Lower Keyford in 1666, and by 1842 the tannery there was run by Charles Case & Son. They remained there until the business was transferred to Westbury about 1920 (where it survived until 1984); their premises have mostly gone now to make way for the Marston Trading Estate, but parts of a few buildings remain. The Frome Chemical Company in Christchurch Street East specialised in making various fertilisers (but were not averse to making things like paint strippers as well!).

Not surprisingly, the 20th Century saw the introduction of a number of new industries to Frome, one of the first of which was rubber production, which was certainly established by Messrs Wallington & Weston by the time of the First World War. They had taken over part of the St John's Mill site at Adderwell, and they made, among other things, solid rubber tyres for both horse-drawn carts and motor cars. Around the time of the Second World War they took over the old Houston & Sons Mill at Vallis Way (which had been damaged by fire). Here they developed a number of sponge rubber products, and also some early plastics (for which the manufacturing processes were somewhat similar to those for rubber). They developed various plastic sheeting products, including cloth- reinforced and electrical insulation sheeting, and an early type of thermoplastic flooring: some of their products were used in the motor industry. However, they did not have sufficient capital to promote many of their products, and in 1956 they were taken over by the Marley Company. Rubber production ceased immediately, but plastic tiles, sheetings, and the Marleyfold doors were produced here, but in 1977 Wallington & Weston joined with an ICI operation to form Weston Hyde. Much of Houstons premises was demolished in 1964, and some of the later Marley buildings have also gone, but other industrial units, as well as the Post Office Sorting Centre, now occupy part of their site.

Another newcomer, also to the St John's Mill site, was Messrs W Pinchin & Co, paint manufacturers, who were subsequently bought out by Cuprinol, the makers of timber preservatives and other products: this firm remained on the site until their Frome operation closed down right at the beginning of the 21st Century. Other industrial concerns in the town which started up in the 20th Century were a number of machinists and tool makers, including Thomson Machine & Tool Co, Curtis Engineering (who made steel frames for agricultural buildings), Stride Metal Works, The County Forge, Wessex Ironcraft, the Somerset Smithy (still active in Christchurch Street West), Frome Tool & Gauge and Wessex Engineering (makers of quarrying and civil engineering machinery).

This chapter should not close without reference to some of the smaller firms which came and went in Frome, particularly in the 19th and 20th Centuries, and these represent a considerable variety. Two of these were connected with the church: there was Prosser the organ builder, for instance: his shop was in the Market Place between the George Hotel and the former Crown Inn: well established by the end of the 19th Century, the shop closed about 1930, but the business continued under a Mr Lambert (who was organist at Berkley Church, and maintained this and other Prosser organs until his death in the 1980s) who relocated to Prosser's workshops in Eagle Lane. There was also a stained glass studio run by the Horwood Brothers in Bridge Street. As well as producing windows for both St John's and St Mary's Churches in Frome, their products were to be found in many churches both in this country and abroad, including churches in Sri Lanka, Sydney and New South Wales in Australia, and there is also a complete set of their windows in Gibraltar Cathedral.

There were many blacksmiths and farriers as mentioned above, and there were saddlers and harness-makers (from Joseph Green, who built 20 and 21 Bath Street in 1815/16, through to Allards of Christchurch Street West, who closed in the 1990s). There were sawmills (one was located at The Butts); and another, which was water powered, was in Spring Gardens (and still working until the 1970s). There was a sail-maker and marine stores which survived in Selwood Road until after the Second World War (I hardly think there could have been much demand for their wares locally!). There were ropeworks (by tradition, one was located at Nos 2-4 Rodden Road, where there is a common loft which could have been so used), tinplate makers, and so on.

Since the Second World War, a new area devoted to industry has been developed in Frome, the Marston Trading Estate, on which a number of engineering firms established premises, as well as a dairy, garages and car service firms, and several large warehouses, including the refrigerated warehouses of Messrs J R Harding and Sons Ltd. This estate was extended in the 1990s into Wessex Fields, where a number of new premises have been constructed, including the present Singers' factory and some small industrial units primarily intended as starter units for new users. At the edge was a conference facility, and large shops for Halfords and Homebase, and a Sainsbury's supermarket, as well as one of the ubiquitous McDonald's outlets. This area too is now nearly fully developed; Coalway Lane on the Eastern side of the town is being developed.

There are also some other buildings locally which must have been used as workshops or small industrial premises in their time, for which I have not been able to find any details, including 44 The Butts (dated 1700, with some workshops attached). There is the building between Cork Street and Catherine Hill (in the grounds of Monmouth House, by tradition an old candle factory, but recently converted into a house called The Wool House). Nos 12-13 Gould's Ground have a structure and ceiling height which suggests a former industrial use.

It seems that Frome has reached a period of change in its local industry with the closing of at least two major firms right at the end of the 20th Century, and one awaits with interest the arrival of new industry in the town representative of the 21st Century!

FOOTNOTES

1.  Rodney Goodall: "The Industries of Frome": Frome Society for Local Study, 2009
2.  Peter Belham: "The Making of Frome": Frome Society for Local Study, 1973
3.  Michael McGarvie: "Frome Through the Ages": Frome Society for Local Study, 1982
4.  Harvey and others: "The Frome Almanack": various (yearly) volumes
5.  Ken Ponting: "Wool & Water": Moonraker Press, 1975 (a good source of information on the woollen industry not only for Frome, but for Trowbridge, Bradford on Avon, Warminster, Westbury and the general district).
6.  Peter Belham: Op. cit.
7.  Anne Partridge: "Frome Selwood": an article in "Somerset & Wessex Life", June 1973 issue
8.  Ken Ponting: Op. cit.
9.  Peter Belham: Op. cit.
10. Ken Ponting: Op. cit.
11. Samuel Cuzner: "Cuzner's Handbook to Froome Selwood": Cuzner, 1866
12. Peter Belham: Op. cit.

13. Identified from the Ordnance survey 1:500 scale map of Frome, published in 1886. In over twenty sheets, an incredible amount of detail is shown: every lamppost and letterbox, pumps, trees, and even garden layouts. Reproduced by Frome Society for Local Study, 2011

14. Peter Belham: Op. cit.

15. White: "A Short History of Frome": publisher unknown, 1892

16. Peter Belham: Op. cit.

17. Peter Belham: Op. cit.

## FORMER SELWOOD PRINTING WORKS, SELWOOD ROAD

Joseph Chapman jr's temple of industry for Messrs Butler and Tanner, now converted into flats.

## CHEAP STREET

Some of the gables of basically late mediaeval houses. (A R Yeates)

## CHURCH STEPS AND CHURCH STREET
More houses with basically pre-1600 origins.

## KEYFORD:THE 18TH CENTURY SHOPFRONT
The only survivor of its kind in Frome.

## LOWER BATH STREET, FROM THE MARKET PLACE
The new "South approach" to Frome, formed between 1810 and 1816.

# CHAPTER SEVEN

# THE COMMERCIAL BUILDINGS OF FROME

Because they form a separate, and rather extensive, category, I am not including the hotels, inns and public houses in this chapter, but in that following. Like the other commercial buildings of the town, they strongly reflect Frome's social history, but also, like them, they are subject to rather more frequent change, as businesses thrive or go under, and as public taste changes.

As one would expect, the earliest commercial buildings are to be found in or near the Market Place, and in those streets linking the Market Place with the main church of St John, particularly King Street and Cheap Street. As it happens, the Market Place was radically altered at the start of the 19th Century, and only the George Hotel, the Crown Inn and the Blue Boar are of a substantially older date than this. The Market Place was originally in two halves, the Upper and Lower Markets, and according to the plan now in Frome Museum, there were two more houses between what is now the HSBC Bank site and the fronts of the George Hotel and the Crown Inn, leaving a gap of rather less than 30 feet between the buildings. The changes were all part of a whole series of modifications to the town centre envisaged by the visionary Thomas Bunn; who, always seeking to make Frome as attractive as the "upstart Bath" just up the road, wanted to convert the Market Place into a Greek agora, using only the best Georgian architecture. Largely as a result of Bunn's initiative. North Parade had been formed as a bypass to Bridge Street in 1797, and Bath Street was cut through a swathe of decrepit buildings from 1810 onwards: the widening of the Market Place completed a radical overhaul of the main road across the town from Shepton Mallet to Bath, cutting out a whole series of bottlenecks, just as what we now know as Christchurch Streets East and West had done with the Radstock to Warminster route almost 100 years earlier.

Cheap Street, however, is quite another matter, and even in 1830, when W W Wheatley did a painting of the street, it was viewed in a somewhat romantic light[1]. (The Frome Society for Local Study acquired an 1835 version of this picture in 2005.) Apart from Nos 9 and 10, and No 17 opposite, which were destroyed by the celebrated Cheap Street fire of 1923, there have been remarkably few changes since the painting was made, other than to the shopfronts in this street. Cheap Street - the street of the chapmen, or merchants - is first referred to as such in a document of 1500, when a butcher bought a vacant plot of land on which a house had stood formerly near the end of "Le Chipstrete" to build his shop. This suggests that the plots in Cheap Street are of a very early date, and were well established by 1500, although one or two have been doubled-up over the years. As might be expected, a street with shops having houses over them was very "middle class" for the 15th/ 16th Centuries, and the properties were probably far better built than the more humble houses of the town. The fact that so many buildings in this street exhibit 16th and 17th Century architectural details suggests that the street was last reshaped to any major extent as the woollen industry in the town really began to prosper, rather than as the result of any dramatic incident, such as a town fire (a not infrequent happening in towns where the buildings were of timber frame construction, but no records having been found of such an occurrence here). Even so, not all of the houses are of stone construction - many are still timber framed. Mercifully, the street has never been accessible for motor vehicles, thanks in part to the stream which runs up the middle, and this has been a major factor in its preservation.

It is probably easiest to consider this street in sequence, rather than in any chronological way, and numerically we can start with the northern side, which is the less altered side. No 1 is the exception: it is of red brick which is quite alien to the town centre, and built c1900 probably for Vincents the Jewellers, who only ceased trading in the town in 1999. They certainly moved across from No 20 Cheap Street shortly after 1904. The building may have been intended as a foil to the c1820 building which stood on the site of the current HSBC Bank, which was a 3-storey, five-bay house constructed of necessity on a possibly reduced site after the widening of the Market Place[2]. In contrast, No 2 has a Georgian style façade of 1820/1830 applied to an earlier building, and this may well have reflected the elevations of the house on the bank site. No 3 also has classical pretensions, but this would seem to be a complete rebuild of the mid-19th Century: the evidence of the rear elevation to Apple Alley supports this hypothesis.

No 4 Cheap Street is the first really interesting building, being of timber-framed, jettied construction, probably 16th Century, but rendered on the front so that it is not so readily appreciated. The shopfront is that installed by the Home and Colonial Stores, presumably when they moved in sometime between 1905 and 1911. The first floor oriel windows, with ovolo mouldings to mullions and transomes, could be as late as 1650 and are probably additions: the top window is a Yorkshire or horizontal sliding sash probably another 100 years younger. The rear is rather more impressive, with a double jetty which gives a much better idea of the original construction (instance the size of the timber corbels - nothing was left to chance then!) and reinforcing the view of a 16th Century dating (although sight of the roof frame might be the final confirmation). The basement and ground floor windows, however, seem to be of the same date as the front oriel window, as indeed is the internal staircase. So, one is left with the possibilities of either a c1550 building with a major reshaping of about 1650, or a total rebuild of 1625, or a few years either way.

No 5 is a rather humbler building by comparison, and yet it also has 16th and 17th Century origins, despite the radical 20th Century alterations to the front. No 6 is also of the same period, although again much altered: one of its most interesting features, for a town house, is the pigeon loft at the rear over the first floor (pigeons normally being bred for food, but this is a feature rather more often found in country houses rather than in a town). No 7/7A is one of the larger properties, possibly originally a double plot. It has a timber-framed front probably of the 16th Century, but the rear is in stone, possibly a later rebuild. This was once the White Hart Inn. The interior has been considerably modified. No 8 also has earlier origins, but is again much altered: only a few traces of 17th Century work remain. The next two properties are the rebuilds following the 1923 fire. It would seem, from the way that they burnt down, that Nos 9 and 10 were also of timber-framed construction, although unlike most of the other houses in this row the ridges to the roofs ran parallel, not at right angles, to the street. The replacements are unashamedly fake half-timbering, which although fashionable at the time, does also suggest that they replace timber-framed buildings. The firemen did well to contain the blaze (which also consumed No 17 opposite when the front of one house fell in): it would have been a very tragic loss if No 11 had also been burnt down.

No 11 Cheap Street is the most sophisticated of Frome's surviving timber-framed buildings, and would stand up in comparison with any such building anywhere in the country. The timber frame is rather more elaborately carved and part decorated, and probably built between 1530 and 1560 (which poses the question - are the others nearby, which are generally coarser in detail, earlier, or debased later, examples?). Again the house is wider, possibly occupying two original plots. The Cheap Street façade has been altered over the years: there is a c1900 shopfront under a stone-tiled pentice, and at first floor level there is an interesting shallow oriel window tucked in under the second floor jetty. The lights of this window are very narrow, and suggest that they could be pre-glass (because glass was so expensive in earlier days, waxed linen was often stretched over windows to exclude the elements but admitting a translucent light: cow's horn, shaved very thin, was another option - one such window survives internally in a house in Milborne Port, Somerset). This theory is given added weight by the presence of internal iron bars, which were more likely used to brace the infill rather than for security purposes, given the width of the lights in the first place. A 2-light early 16th Century window, now blocked up, is said to remain in a side wall. At first floor level inside is a splendid stone fireplace - a little unusual for Frome, as we shall see later - but several experts have accepted it as being 15th Century rather than a sympathetic 19th Century insertion, despite the excellent condition which makes me a little suspicious. The circular stone stair has been modified, and a rather pretty rear office with 18th and 19th Century details has been removed in recent years. This was obviously a house for someone of considerable local standing, but as yet little has been uncovered regarding its early owners or occupiers.

No 12 makes an interesting contrast: it is of late 18th or early 19th Century date, with classical detailing and a nicely worked corner: it appears to have been amended at the rear in c1850. This completes the north side of Cheap Street (and incidentally gives us a glance at Apple Alley, which runs up the back of these properties: this is well worth a visit: apart from the early stone pavings which add to the character, the backs of some of these houses are as interesting as their fronts - in some cases more so). It is instructive to look at the levels of some of the door thresholds comparative to the surface of Apple Alley: the threshold to No 4, for instance, which is now some 2 feet (600mm) below modern ground level (whereas there was probably once a small step up to prevent water penetration to the interior) shows clearly how soil and ground levels tend to rise over the centuries compared with the internal floor levels.

On the other side of the street, opposite No 12 is No 13, by tradition and repute the oldest house in Frome. This reputation may in part be due to its strange form, due to the shape of the site forming a sharp angle with Eagle Lane, but although much of the external timberwork is manifestly a replacement, it does follow the form of the building as depicted in the earliest known illustrations, going back at least 150 years. Again, this was a jettied building, although here only of two-storeys. There remains a 17th Century timber window on the Cheap Street façade, and it is said that another old window was found elsewhere in the building, but covered up again. No 14 is a modest building apparently all of stone: the Venetian window suggests a date of the late 18th Century, but the core of the building is earlier, as the clearly 17th Century doorway would suggest. This is one of the few buildings in the street retaining front access to its cellar (on the other side of the street, of course, access was at the rear, due to the fall of the land).

No 15, despite its false half-timbered front, is of about 1600 or so, as was revealed when it was converted into a bakery in the 1980s. Previously it had served for many years as Frome's fish shop: Alfred Vincent, the proprietor of the shop at the beginning of the 20th Century, who appears in many photographs and postcards, used to keep his fish (but hopefully not his chickens) fresh by frequently washing them in the stream in front of the shop. The Vincent family ran this shop from about 1840 to about 1930, when it was taken over by MacFisheries (now the Bakery). No 16 was, until about 1911, the Albion Inn; it then became what contemporary sources described as a "coffee tavern", and has continued to develop from a modest cafe until it has become a restaurant of considerable repute. The fabric here is mostly of 17th and 18th Century, but the first floor had a 19th Century remodelling, and the Albion Room (named after a former public house), at the rear (abutting Eagle Lane) was refurbished in the 1980s.

No 17, which is in stone, is a complete rebuild following the 1923 fire. The blaze which destroyed its predecessor must have generated considerable heat, because forest marble, like many building stones, turns pink when exposed to great heat: both Nos 16 and 18 bear the scars of that fire to this day, if one looks carefully. No 18 is probably of a late 18th Century date, but with some 19th Century modifications, as is the neighbouring property, the rather narrower No 19. No 20 occupies a double plot, and appears to be a complete rebuild from ground floor upwards of about 1850 or 1860; however, the cellars are much earlier, and bear no relationship to the walls above them.

No 21 has a 19th Century façade, but much of the fabric behind is of an older house, and No 22 would seem to be at least mid-18th Century, in that it seems to tally with a lease from Lord Cork of Marston House to a Thomas Maynard in 1752. It may be small, but it is significant as having the only surviving stone slated roof (albeit heavily torched with cement) in the town centre: this must have been the prevailing material before the advent of the railways brought cheaper Welsh slate and Bridgwater clay tiles to the town. Nos 23 and 24 are early 19th Century buildings, of pleasant character outside but much modified internally. This brings us to Lloyds TSB Bank, which I will deal with together with the Market Place buildings.

Outside Cheap Street there remain few early shops, although we must remember that the "front room" of many houses served as a shop until comparatively recent times, especially if the house stood on a corner: some such 19th Century shopfronts exist in the houses of the high pavements of Palmer Street and Paul Street. In former days the need for a window display was hardly considered necessary. There is one charming exception, however: at No 25 Keyford we have what is probably Frome's only 18th Century shopfront. The building appears to be of about 1750, with a Mansard pattern roof, so the shopfront could be part of the original building. It has a pair of 20-pane bow windows with central door and fanlight which would be a credit to any shop: it is perhaps ironic that the shop became a very modern video hire shop before reverting to a private house!

The only other bow windows of which I am aware in Frome are to No 25 Vicarage Street, (although I can find no mention of this serving as a shop during the 20th Century: this window is in fact a copy of a 19th Century window which suffered from neglect and vandalism when the property was empty for many years in the 1950s and 1960s) and one in Whittox Lane. No other 18th Century shops, in a recognisable form, have come down to us. (It is worth mentioning, in passing, that Frome had several markets, including the important market in what is now Trinity Street, which served the Newtown area of Frome until all the markets were amalgamated in 1875.)

However, once we enter the 19th Century we have many shops to consider, and chronologically it might be best to start with Bath Street. This was cut through following the Frome Turnpike Act of 1810: Thomas Bunn, writing some years later, just before he died, remarks:

"This town was one of the worst, if not the very worst, in the County of Somerset. The thoroughfares mere lanes, so narrow that carriages could not pass each other without ascending the footways. In 1810, after having conversed about improvements the previous twenty years, an Act of Parliament was passed for that and other purposes. The streets of Bath measured, and, omitting those which were built for splendour of an hundred feet wide, Union Street was adopted as a model for convenience, the space for the carriage road being twenty six feet, and each footway seven feet, in the whole forty feet. Of this breadth the new roads have been made at Frome. There was necessarily an excavation of the road, sixteen feet in depth. The dunghills and other offences were removed, and on the banks adjoining the new roads, shrubs and flowers were planted. The architecture was improved, particularly the West front and Gateway of the parish church, designed by Sir Jeffrey Wyattville[3]."

Bunn talks rather grandly of roads in the plural, but in fact only Bath Street (named after Lord Bath, on whose land most of the new street was constructed) was formed under this Act. The excavations seem excessive, although this must have been the case in one or two places: it should also be remembered that some of the lower Bath Street properties have cellars which extend under the pavement, and possibly out into the road in places, just as many of the Georgian properties in Bath have, which might explain the extra depth.

The creation of Bath Street involved the demolition of some rather unsavoury premises in what was known as Anchor Barton, and also the houses on the east side of Rook Lane (the original Rook Lane ran uphill from the corner of Palmer Street, across the front of Rook Lane Chapel and along the front of Rook Lane House, now a little way along Christchurch Street West - the present Rook Lane merely perpetuates the name). The whole of lower Bath Street was new building, mostly of 1810-1816, although the corner premises (where the Coventry Building Society now stands), formed part of the Upper Market Place, and remained, to be rebuilt later. The upper part of Bath Street was laid out as a fair approach into the town: there was greenery on both sides (including two magnificent Cedars of Lebanon planted in 1815, one of which died at the beginning of

68

the 20th Century, but the other still survives), and neat stone walls with fielded piers and railings on top (the railings being removed during the Second World War). With Thomas Bunn as one of the promoters of the scheme, the new buildings had to be in the Greek idiom. They were almost certainly architect-designed, but the name of the architect is lost: it could have been John Pinch of Bath, who was practising by 1800, and who designed elevations for the George Hotel and attached Assembly Rooms (now the Natwest Bank) for Bunn in 1819, or George Underwood, the County Surveyor, who designed Christ Church in 1817 and the buildings on The Bridge in 1820.

The north-east corner of the Market Place and Bath Street also had to be rebuilt, as this was where the new access into the Market Place was formed. The building at No 1 Bath Street was a little later than the rest, being built about 1835, but the design is consistent with the lower Bath Street elevations. For forty years it was the establishment of Aldhelm Ashby (1882-1958) a photographer, many of whose works survive as postcards of the town, and traces of signwriting promoting his business still survive on the ashlar walling. No 2 Bath Street (subdivided into two separate premises now) is also slightly later: it was rebuilt by Stuckeys Bank (again with an unknown designer, but obviously under Bunn's influence) in 1835. It remained a bank until 1923, when, after several mergers, it became part of the then Westminster Bank. In 1927 the Frome Selwood Permanent Building Society moved here from 21 King Street, and remained here until 1970, when they took over the premises of the old National Provincial Bank, which had also merged with the Westminster Bank to form the National Westminster (now abbreviated to Natwest).

Nos 3-8 Bath Street were part of the original Bath Street Scheme, and appear to be of one build, (not surprisingly as they were on land forming part of the Longleat Estate, which must have made the clearing of the site for the new street much easier). It may be that the development was speculative: it was certainly not very solidly constructed: the 3-storey front walls are only 150mm (6") solid masonry, and rely on the concavity on plan for their strength. Nos 3 and 8 needed stiffening considerably in the 1960s to ensure the stability of the group. Interestingly, the party - and rear walls (in rubble stone) are much thicker, and it may be that some portions of the previous buildings on the site were incorporated into the new work. The façade of No 4 (which was originally the Anchor Inn, facing onto Cox or Cocks Street (Eagle Lane), with the opening and inserted Ionic columns, was amended fairly early in the present building's history, certainly by 1835. The first occupier was John Sinkins, a draper (who may be either the same, or a relative of, the John Sinkins who became a prominent 19th Century clothier in the town, building a major house at Wallbridge and also the Literary and Scientific Institution in North Parade). No 6 was the town's Post Office from 1864 (having moved from Vicarage Street) until 1914; No 7 was a printing establishment with bookshop for many years; and No 8 (of which the writer occupied the upper floors for his offices for 20 years) is graced with a cartouche on the corner which features the Thynne coat of arms - an acknowledgement that it was through Lord Bath, the principal landowner concerned, that Bath Street was constructed.

The forecourt to St John's Church was cleared, demolishing The Bell Inn (there was another Bell Inn in Trinity Street) and some other properties: the house looking onto the forecourt on the north side, and which belongs to St John's Church, is a replacement house of c1925.

Argyll Chambers, on the uphill side of the forecourt, is actually a 19th Century addition to Argyll House, in Gentle Street; it was an attorney's offices by 1835, and has remained as solicitors' offices ever since. Above this, the remaining premises are domestic and will be described later. Across the street, on the corner of Bath Street and Palmer Street, Nos 16 and 17 Bath Street were commercial premises for many years before being converted for the Frome Board of Guardians in 1837 (the year after they were established to administer the Poor Law) and remained as such until their new offices in Christchurch Street West were finished in 1891. For a while the premises were an auction mart, but in 1930 they were radically reshaped to become the local Tax, Customs and Excise offices; the tax offices remained there until 1948, the Customs & Excise until about 1974. The St John Ambulance Divisional Office was opened in 1948 in the old tax office; the remainder reverted to commercial premises in 1974.

The opposite corner of Bath Street was occupied by a Palmer Street house which had been unaffected by the road works, its garden flanking the street: possibly about 1834 a shop opening onto Bath Street was built to the rear of the house. The Longleat Estate sold the lease of the house and shop in 1919, and the Co-operative Society, who already owned premises in Palmer Street adjoining this house, purchased the site, demolished the house and shop and erected the present building in 1923/24, to the design of Percy Rigg, the local architect who had an office in Cork Street. It is very much representative of its date, relatively progressive in its use of fenestration, although Rigg maintained that "the idea which had been kept in view was that the new buildings should be somewhat in harmony with the old"! These houses have now been renovated sympathetically.

No 19 Bath Street (Devon House) was built shortly after 1814, and had a chequered career as a grocers, a boarding school and cabinet maker, but by 1860 was being referred to as a "music salon" where pianos were bought and sold, and music taught by the proprietor, John Cox, a leading light in Frome's music scene. In 1910 the premises were amalgamated with No 19A, which is of the same build, to become a butcher's shop: the glazed ceramic shopfront dates from this time: the business continued under several owners until the mid-1990s. Nos 20 and 21 replace a warehouse, stables and outbuildings in the former Anchor Barton, and were completed by 1816. No 20 was a pharmacy for over 150 years from at least 1820 to 1974 (some of the fittings are now in Frome Museum), but has had various uses since then. No 21 also had a long period serving one type of business - that of watchmaker/ jeweller: George Ballard moved here in 1848, and he was here until he died in 1902; his son continued until 1919, and the business was sold to Charles Hart, whose firm still trades in Frome, having moved from here to Cheap Street in the 1970s. No 22 is another c1816 building, and the upper floors have served as solicitors' offices since 1849, although the firm occupying them, Messrs Daniel & Cruttwell, now FDC Law, is much older, with a continuous history of some 300 years, embracing the Wickham family, one of whose members was instrumental in getting the Blue House built. However, the ground floor remained as a shop until 1985.

The next building, The Wheatsheaf (or Mansford & Baily, as it was known for many years), will be dealt with in the next chapter. No 24, although not part of the Longleat Estate (which covered the remainder of the new Bath Street), also had a property which had to be demolished to enable the new road to be built, and a new house was built here for Edward Cockey by 1823 (presumably so that he could live near his foundry further up the road). The premises may have remained as a house until 1919 (but linked with the business carried on from 1 Market Place next door), when Edwin York opened a motor car repairing and building business here, and the ground floor became a garage/ workshop which remained until the 1960s: in 1974 the premises were converted to an estate agency, which although having had several changes of owner, remains to the present time. This now brings us to the Market Place.

The Market Place may reasonably be assumed to represent the heart of Frome, and there is no reason to suppose that the town's principal market has been held anywhere else since the Domesday survey, albeit in two sections until the whole Market Place was opened-up in the early 19th Century. Indeed, the selling of cattle took place here in front of what became the old Post Office until the end of the 19th Century, when it moved into what is still called the Market Yard (originally a field for the watering and fattening-up of cattle after they had been walked into Frome - a practice which survived until after the writer moved to Frome in 1963 - which field was also the original site of the Frome Show) until the Frome Cattle Market was relocated to Standerwick Farm, at Berkley, in 1990. There is still a token market in the Market Place held every Wednesday and Saturday, even though the bulk of the market is now in the Market Yard. Of the buildings at the top end, there are the old Burton's the Tailors building, of the 1930s, and the former bank, now the Coventry Building Society designed by W.G.Brown, which dates from 1911.

On the upper corner of Stony Street/Cork Street, opposite the building Society, is the 1950s building occupied by Barclays Bank. This was the site of a draper's shop, Fear Hill, who occupied a Georgian building which, sadly, endured the indignity of receiving several motor vehicles impacting into it, their brakes having failed whilst descending Bath Street, and eventually there were some fears for its safety and it was demolished. On the opposite corner is part of Thomas Bunn's dream "Agora": the Assembly Room of c 1820, with the covered market underneath (as already described in Chapter 5), and then the George Hotel and Crown Inn, which are discussed in the following chapter. Nos 7 and 8 Market Place seem to be of the late 17th or early 18th Century, judging from their rear elevations; it seems that they were originally a single house, but divided into two and refronted between 1830 and 1840. Then comes the former Post Office, converted from the former Bull's Temperance Hotel and opened in 1914, replacing the Bath Street offices, and which closed in 2004. The premises now occupied by Messrs Boots, and the adjoining shops, are basically later 19th Century buildings. The shop on the opposite corner of Scott Road, built for, and occupied by Messrs Halfords until they relocated to Wessex Fields in 1999, replaced a fine 5-bay Georgian house built for Wilkins the Salter prior to 1719, and was erected just before the Second World War[4].

Scott Road (named after a local County Councillor and former chairman of the Frome Urban District Council who had garage premises in what was once the Blue Boar Yard), is largely a 1950s/ 1960s development: the premises occupied by the Ellenbray Press were built as the Frome Library about 1966, to the design of Vallis and Vallis, the Frome architects.

71

On the other side of the Market Place, Woolworths replaced Newports (later Suttons) antiques and furniture removers business, presumably in the 1930s, and, in their turn by Iceland; the rest of this side up to King Street is occupied by Dungarvan Buildings (named after the heir to the Earl of Cork and Orrery, of Marston, who was then still Lord of the Manor of Frome): these were built by Henry Miller, a solicitor, sportsman and entrepreneur who lived at Welshmill House in 1850. (The row was built in a vaguely classical style, but presumably Miller had not been Thomas Bunn's best friend since he built his own offices in Cork Street, next door but one to Bunn's own house, in an emphatically Gothic style in 1842!). Then, on the other side of King Street, comes the HSBC Bank (formerly the Midland Bank, who built this replacement building about 1920). Lloyds Bank building was erected about 1840, originally for the Wilts and Dorset Bank, although it was considerably altered, if not rebuilt, in 1874 to the designs of W J Stent. No 25 ties in with the construction of Bath Street in the early 19th Century, although it was considerably modified later in that century, possibly by Joseph Singer.

The first part of the 20th Century brought considerable changes to Palmer Street and Stony Street, where one side of each street was totally rebuilt in the period 1900 to 1930 or so. Along the north side of Palmer Street, the Co-operative Society had purchased most of the former properties there and demolished them to make way for a variety of buildings of different dates. The Co-op had been in Frome since before 1900, and in 1912/13 they decided to rebuild their main premises. The centre block, (formerly their grocery stores with an assembly hall over for shareholders meetings) was finished by the end of 1913 and formally opened on 4th April 1914. The building was designed by a Mr Harris (possibly of Bristol) and built by a Mr Parsons. The gap between this building and the Bath Street Corner building of 1923 remained open until the 1950s, when the current buildings were added. The red brick department store on the Palmer Street/ Stony Street corner is of the 1930s: this totally inappropriate building was owned by the New Day Furnishing Company. There is then a variety of mostly 1930s premises down the East side of Stony Street. However, on the other side, some of the properties are much older: the current hairdressing salon on the upper corner is of the Regency Period, and Nos 16/17 were formerly one rather grand house. There remains to the latter a fine rear staircase in a separate stair turret with a pyramidal roof, some fine rear leaded windows, and a rainwater hopperhead dated 1688. You have to look more closely at the front elevation at the upper levels to see that once the windows had architraves with pediments - but these have been shaved off, and the former pitched roof has gone to be replaced with a flat one. (This perhaps reinforces the fact that to understand Frome buildings, it is just as, if not more important, to look at the backs of the buildings, where there have been less alterations over the years - all too often the façades were renewed, giving a false impression of the age of the building.)

The other (minor) shopping streets in Frome are King Street, Palmer Street, Paul Street, Stony Street, Catherine Hill and Catherine Street, with other rows of shops in Christchurch Streets East and West, Badcox and Vallis Way, and more isolated shops in Keyford, the Trinity Area, and along The Butts, but most of the shops are adapted houses rather than purpose-built shops, and a number have been converted back to houses. In several cases the core of the building is earlier than 1800, but the shopfronts, where they survive, are mostly of the 19th Century. Some represented the typical "corner shop", but others were designed to catch passing trade, and it is worth considering, for a moment, the normal traffic routes through the town, particularly prior to the creation of Bath Street. For those travelling from Bristol via Radstock through to Warminster and Southampton (now the A362) they would have come along Vallis Way to Badcox, and then gone down Catherine Street and Catherine Hill, across Palmer Street (originally part of Stony Street), across to the south of St John's Church to use Church Walk or Twattle Alley into what is now Vicarage Street (or up Gentle Street) and then to the Portway. Behind Town (what we now know as Christchurch Streets East and West) was a mid 18th Century additional toll road which bypassed the town avoiding the dips down and back up again, (although many would have taken the old route to avoid paying the toll) and there was little building to the south of this road before 1800.

To cross the town using the route from Shepton Mallet to Bath and Trowbridge (formerly the A361, now the B3090) one would come along the Ridgeway at Marston, and along The Butts to Gorehedge, then round to the top of Rook Lane, going down to the junction with Palmer Street, (or if on foot, via Gentle Street and Cheap Street) and then via Stony Street into the Market Places, Upper and Lower; then via Bridge Street (the last developed road in the town there were few buildings on this side of the river then) into what is now Welshmill Road and along the river to Spring Gardens and Beckington. The creation of Bath Street eliminated a major congestion point and accident black spot on the corner of Palmer Street (where many downhill travelling carts came to grief). It is perhaps surprising that so many shops on the old through roads survived so many years after the passing trade dwindled - in some cases, such as Catherine Hill and Street, they were helped by the new developments of housing around the edge of the old town which generated a more local "passing trade".

As we have seen, comparatively few buildings in Frome were intended purely as shops: even the purpose-built row of shops at Badcox (dating from c1890, and one of the earliest, and most intrusive, use of bricks in the town) had apartments over them. The two main shopping precincts in the town are of the second half of the 20th Century. The first was the Westway Precinct, developed by the Commercial Union Insurance Company in conjunction with the Frome Urban District Council, who had assembled the land. Designed by Messrs William Saunders of Southampton, it was completed in 1973. The site was principally that occupied by Hall House, a Georgian House demolished in 1934 which had gardens running down to the river: The Gaumont Cinema was built on part of the site in the 1930s, and the rest was developed during the Second World War when concrete huts housing the Food Office and suchlike were put up as temporary buildings. The local health clinic was also situated here until the Park Road Health Centre was built. The original designs for the precinct met with considerable criticism locally, and the executed scheme is a bit of a compromise: perhaps the worst element was the use of a very dark brick said to match in with the local stonework - unfortunately most of the stonework in the town centre has been cleaned since then! Some modifications and improvements were made to the centre in 1998, in anticipation of a continuing development across the river, but this has yet to materialise!

The other central shopping development is the Kingsway Precinct, developed off King Street by L R Ings, and opened in 1976: here the architecture, quite uncompromising towards Frome, did at least use reconstructed stone, but in a Ham stone colour appropriate to Yeovil, not Frome! In the outskirts of the town, one or two purpose built shops have been erected to serve local trade: these include the Spar shop at Keyford, the local shops in Critchill and Packsaddle, and the row of shops in Forest Road on the Stonebridge Estate. Then in the 1990s edge-of-town shopping came to Frome, with the erection of Sainsbury's store at Marston which opened in 1993, and, opposite, the Homebase and Halfords stores which opened in 1999. As has been the case with other towns, this had a marked effect on the shops in the town centre, and another out-of-town shopping development proposed for Wallbridge met with stiff opposition, and although initially conditional planning consent was granted (subject to the creation of a flood relief scheme), there were second thoughts, and much in-fighting before the scheme was finally allowed. The new Asda supermarket opened here in 2005. To redress the town centre balance, a Lidl store was opened in Garston Lane in 1999, and there are proposals for the development of Merchants Barton as a shopping precinct, which will extend the scope of the town centre as well as adding more parking space. It will be interesting to see how this, and other commercial aspects of Frome, develop in the future.

FOOTNOTES

1.   Picture illustrated in "The Blue House Restored": Blue House Appeal Committee, 1965

2.   Michael McGarvie: "Frome in Old Picture Postcards", Volume 2: European library, 1984

3.   Derek Gill: "Experiences of a 19th Century Gentleman": Frome Society for Local Study, 2003

4.   Michael McGarvie: "The Book of Frome": Barracuda Books, 1980

For much of the other detail in this chapter I am indebted to Francis Kelly, and the Statutory List descriptions of the buildings concerned, and to the directory sections of various volumes of the Frome Almanack.

# CHAPTER EIGHT
# THE INNS AND HOSTELRIES OF FROME

On the 1774 map of Frome some forty three inns are marked as being within Frome (some, on the perimeter, such as the Royal Oak at Cottles Oak were not included). Of these, some nine are still open for business, and the premises of a further eleven are clearly identifiable. In addition, those outside the scope of the map which probably existed by 1774 include, as well as the Royal Oak, the Crown at Keyford, the Vine Tree, and possibly the Halfway House at Clink. The survivors are the Angel (now the Archangel after a major refurbishment) and the Three Swans (King Street), the George, Crown and Blue Boar (Market Place), the Griffin (Milk Street), the Crown & Sceptre (Trinity Street, known in 1774 as the Jolly Butcher), the Lamb and Fountain (Castle Street), the Pack Horse (Christchurch Street West), and the Ship (now the Olive Tree, at Badcox), so there are at least 12 pre-1774 inns in the town.

It is not easy to sort out which is Frome's oldest inn, but the location and the names (being pre-reformation - religious names went out of vogue after the 1530s) would suggest that it would be either the George or the Angel. (The former has a recorded history going back before the Hanoverian period, so it is named after the saint, not the king.) A former landlord of the Angel was adamant that his inn had 14th Century origins, and it has the right kind of location, off the Market Place, and form (an entrance gateway with through yard for carriages now being clearly in evidence), but it has been so modified over the years that there are only a few 18th Century fragments, including the entrance gates. Purely in architectural terms, the Three Swans just up the road could well be the oldest actual structure: its entrance door frame, if not the door, could be of the later 16th Century, and the centre part is certainly a timber-framed building with a street gable: the nature of the roof frame could be decisive in determining the actual date. There are radical internal alterations, however, and it has been extended on both sides.

The George is the first inn to be recorded, in 1650, and was one of the properties belonging to the Manor of Frome. The rear elevation is certainly suggestive of a 17th Century date, but the remainder has been remodelled on several occasions. The first recorded works were in 1754/55, when the ownership changed to a new Lord of the Manor, the Boyle family of Marston. There were plans for new stables, etc. in 1813, but these came to nothing at that time. In 1819/20 the Assembly Room and covered market was built next door (in what had been Thomas Bunn's garden), and before long these were linked into the George at first floor level, so that they could be serviced from the George. The landlord who took over in 1834 stayed for 40 years, and left the place in a very run down state, necessitating a major overhaul in 1874/75, during which time business was transferred to No 12 Gentle Street. The façade has been little changed since, except for the involuntary removal of the open-pillared porch which was demolished by a runaway lorry during the First World War (a fate also suffered by the Wheatsheaf in Bath Street in the 1970s). However, the place had deteriorated so much by the mid-1970s that it closed again, and was threatened with either demolition or absorption into the bank next door. Fortunately a local restaurant owner, Freddie Giles, restored the hotel and reopened it again as the only hotel in the town centre.

The throughway for carriages, still discernible before the last restoration, was heavily disguised, but the general form was the same as that of the Angel. The George has played a significant part in Frome's history: it was the setting for two election riots, in 1832 and 1854, suffering minor damage as a result of it being used as the polling station. The front balcony was not only used for pre-election speeches from the candidates, but also for the declaration of the election result, as well as other public proclamations[1].

The Crown, next door to the George, (closed for several years, but having undergone restoration as a public house is closed again), was first recorded as "Garret's House" in 1681, but it is not certain whether it was then a public house (which it certainly was by 1774). The sides and rear are of a 17th Century style, but the front is later - possibly as late as the 1820s (after the front had become more prominent following the opening-up of the two halves of the Market Place). The street door had a pedimented surround, but this was shaved off sometime before 1950, leaving a rather plain front. Included inside is a date tablet of 1697 over a first floor fireplace: this might refer to a remodelling rather than a rebuilding (although an oculus window in a rear gable is very typical of the end of the 17th and early 18th Century: it could also be the date in which it became the Crown Inn).

The Blue Boar, at the opposite end of the Market Place, is also late 17th Century, being built by one Theophilus Lacey in 1691. This inn has also suffered much change over the years, and it is not certain how much original fabric survives. This was probably a larger inn than is now suggested: the Blue Boar Yard was on the other side of the Market Place, where Scott Road is now, (surviving into living memory), and suggested that it too, like the Angel and the George, could cope with the coaching and carriage trade[2].

The Crown at Keyford is also almost certainly a 17th Century inn. Built to serve the hamlet of Keyford when it was still detached from Frome, it was also, like the Ring-o-Bells, the Vine Tree, and possibly others a stopping point to water the horses (and whet the whistles of their drivers) after the long hard climb out of Frome. The road here was then the main road out to Longleat (via Woodlands): an important factor, as at least a third of Frome was once part of the Longleat estate. Currently there is no positive dating for the inn, but it is likely on architectural evidence to date from between 1650 and 1700. Although it has suffered the inevitable alterations over the years, it does retain some of its original character.

Two other inns are almost certainly pre-1700; the Royal Oak, at Cottles Oak on the southern outskirts of the town (originally very much a country inn providing a watering-place for those who had toiled up Critchill), and the Ship Inn (currently The Olive Tree), at Badcox, which, when it was built, was right on the outskirts of the pre-1670 town. The Royal Oak, because of its position, may well have been built as an inn, but there are no known records mentioning it: the name is, of course, Carolingian, and the building has all the appearances of a 17th Century origin, although much altered internally. The Ship Inn is also likely to be mid 17th Century, almost certainly being there before the Trinity Area, or Newtown, was commenced about 1665, even though it is first recorded only in 1766.

By about 1700 a number of new inns had appeared. The Trinity Area naturally had a number of public houses, especially along what is now known as Trinity Street, where markets were held: this boasted five inns. Of these, the Lamb and Fountain, actually in Castle Street at the end of Trinity Street, is the least altered, and its ovolo-moulded windows suggest a date rather earlier than 1700: it also has an unusual horizontal sliding sash window (similar to one at 4 Cheap Street), as well as a fine, and surely original, front door. I have never been inside, but it seems to be more like a traditional ale or cider house, where the bar was really the parlour of the house, and the casks were stored in a still room behind - the whole layout being really quite domestic in character. The White Horse at 11 Portway, which closed in 1977, was another such house, where you sat in the "front room" and drinks were served from the kitchen/still room, through a small hatch. It is also important to remember that, prior to about 1960, many of these small inns were not licensed to sell wines or spirits, merely ale and cider: the selling of a full range of alcoholic beverages, and now food to accompany them, is a relatively modern phenomenon. The Crown and Sceptre (originally the Jolly Butcher) is certainly pre-1774 in origin, but has been much altered and is almost unrecognisable as being an early Inn - the façade was rebuilt about 1800, and much of the rear some 100 years later. The Kings Head, on the corner of Trinity Street and Selwood Road, and which certainly looks the part of a cl680 building, closed in the 1960s, and was converted into a house: this had considerable importance, as it was from here that tolls were collected from people going into Frome: accordingly, by holding a market here, on the north west edge of the town, the tolls were avoided. Further along, towards the church, at No 8 was the Bell Inn (shown as being the Talbot Inn on the 1774 map), which also closed in the 1960s: its façade was partially rebuilt, possibly in the 19th Century, and again in the 1970s: it is now converted into flats. The last of the Trinity Street inns was The Trooper, probably where Butler & Tanner's old warehouse now stands.

If this were not sufficient, there was the Griffin in nearby Milk Street, still trading and once again brewing its own beer, (although the fabric is much altered), and almost next door to it was Doctor Andrews ; and on Vallis Way, at No 38, was the Angel and Crown, which closed about 1970 and is now a private house[3]. This does retain some early features, including one in what is a series of Frome fireplaces of the 1680s, although the rear datestone only has the "16" still visible. In Naish's Street, near the corner with Brandy Lane, was the King of Prussia. At the bottom of Fountain Lane (Castle Street) was the Star and Garter, and further up was the Spread Eagle; in Whittox Lane was the Masons' Arms (not to be confused with the inn of the same name on the Marston Road). Just outside the Trinity Area there were the White Swan at Badcox (right on the corner formed by Broadway and Vallis Way, and I believe later removed to Vallis Way outside the old Wallington & Weston Factory), and a little further up Broadway, before you reached the Ring O' Bells, were the Pack Saddle and the Red Lion; further up, nearer the Royal Oak, was the Swan at No 105. Furthermore, on the site of what is now the car park at Badcox was the Woolpack (not to be confused with the Woolpack at 8 Culverhill, Keyford!). All in all, the inhabitants of the Newtown were well watered!

On the other side of the river in Bridge Street (and originally the only inn on that side until you reached the Vine Tree), was the Black Swan, which traded until about 1950: it looks more 18th than 17th Century, and is now enjoying a new life as part of an arts and crafts complex. In North Parade was The Champneys Inn, a building of 1739, but not necessarily built as an inn.

Coming into the town centre again there was the Bear in King Street, and the Waggon and Horses in Gentle Street[4], which architecturally seems to be of the 17th Century, but which is first mentioned in 1568. It closed in 1960, and was converted by the Urban District Council into four flats. Because of the topography of the town, this became the main coaching inn for the town once Behind Town had been constructed, because it avoided the need to negotiate the slopes into and out of the town centre. It was from here that "the old standing constant Frome Flying Waggon" started, which for thirty shillings (if you could afford it) would whisk you up to London in a day and a half, with an overnight stop. Its yard, now a private car park for the flats, extended into, and was accessed from, the top of Blindhouse Lane. In the church forecourt was the Bell Inn (not to be confused with the Newtown Bell Inn), the original building of which was cleared away in 1810 or so to make way for the new church forecourt (I believe the Bell Inn continued from 9 Christchurch Street East - Fairlawn House - for a while); and across the road, in Palmer Street, was the Weymouth Arms (which by 1900, possibly after the Longleat estate had sold much of its holding in Frome, became the Bath Arms - Lord Weymouth being the heir to Lord Bath). It was certainly pre-1774, but there is no architectural dating evidence surviving. This remained as an inn until the 1950s, when it was converted into a gift shop, but by the 1980s it had changed into a licensed restaurant and bar - almost back to its original function.

Three other town centre inns which I have mentioned in connection with the shops in Cheap Street and Bath Street were the Albion and the Anchor (Eagle Lane, which itself takes its name from a former inn on the corner of Church Steps) and the White Hart (Cheap Street) - all pre 1774 inns. There was also the Globe in Eagle Lane. On the corner of Stony Street and Catherine Hill was the Fleur de Lys; then in Catherine Hill were the Castle at No 32, and the Wheatsheaves (not to be confused with the Wheatsheaf in Bath Street) at No 22, which survived as an inn well into the 20th Century: it is now a beauty parlour with apartments over, and the side elevation still has an early leaded window; and then further along in Catherine Street was the Anchor at No 29 and then the Sun Inn. The original premises for this latter inn were demolished in 1812 to make way for an extension to the Badcox Lane Baptist Chapel, but it relocated into similar 17th Century premises virtually next door, where it is still in business[5].

Once we come further into the 18th Century, and the construction of the new road "Behind Town", there was a perceived need for another inn, the Pack Horse, which from its slightly quirky façade seems to date from between 1730 and 1750. Like most inns, especially those which belong to brewers, it has been much altered, although some features remain (one has to remember that, like shops, inns need to be periodically updated to keep their trade - and in these days to meet with various Health and Safety standards!). The name is meaningful: in the yard to the rear was a coal merchant, and the pack animals who

78

carried the coal to Frome from the Mells and Radstock coalfields would be unloaded here and then set to graze in the "Bailys or Pack Horse Ground", which in 1817 was to become Christ Church churchyard[6]. This inn, of course, was intended to catch passing through trade; so was the Ring-o-Bells, in what is now Broadway, the road to Mells and Wells, again pre 1774, but bearing little sign of being an early building. On the other side of the town (and when built well out into the country), was the Vine Tree, but this was totally demolished and rebuilt in the 1930s. Even further out, in what was then open countryside, was the Halfway House (Clink Farm), but little is known about this. On the Shepton Mallet Road, just within the boundaries of modern Frome, is the Masons Arms at Marston, which may well have 18th Century origins, and which probably served the masons from Bulls Quarr (or quarry, which was just below the roundabout at the Marston end of the Frome bypass) as they came back to Frome. The current building has some 18th Century character, although much altered at ground floor level. Another 18th Century inn was the Champneys Arms, built somewhere near where the telephone exchange now stands, about 1739. This too survived until the 1950s, but has been demolished since, to make way for offices and new houses. Yet another 18th Century building which became an inn, even if it did not start out as such, was the Unicorn at Keyford, which stood on the site of the present fire station.

Once one reaches the 19th Century, there were a number of new public houses created, mostly rather small in size. One of the earliest, tied in with the newly cleared Market Place and the newly constructed bridge over the River Frome, was the Bridge Hotel, which was presumably part of Underwood's original design for the bridge and the houses thereon. It was probably modified about 1890, and closed in 1972, the premises currently being occupied by the Halifax Building Society and Bank. Amongst the smaller inns were the White Horse in Portway (described above), the Red Lion in The Butts, and the Woolpack at Culverhill, which all closed down in the 1970s; presumably because they were not really suited for the expanded trade in dealing with wines and spirits, and at a time when the demand for pure beer houses had declined substantially. In addition, there were some inns which had a rather shorter life, and which are only known through contemporary directories to the town; these include the Royal Standard at 12 Horton Street, the Dolphin in 62/63 Naish's Street, and the Black Prince in Vicarage Street, as well as a later Anchor at 29 Catherine Hill. Several larger public houses were also built: these include the Beehive in Keyford (which closed soon after 2000), the Victoria in Christchurch Street East (which closed in the early 1980s), and the First and Last (formerly the Railway Inn) down by the station, which is currently a Chinese restaurant.

The 20th Century saw only one new public house (as opposed to rebuilding, as was the case with the Vine Tree); this was the Weaver, (formerly the New Inn) on the corner of The Butts and Somerset Road which is now closed. This was built before 1915, replacing a New Inn recorded at 138 The Butts in 1905. On the other hand, there were two significant conversions of houses into hotels with bars. The first of these was the Portway Hotel, a house of about 1800 converted in 1934 under the direction of Ronald Vallis, the Frome architect: this closed in the late 1980s and is now adapted into flats. In the 1950s the Mendip Lodge, an early 20th Century house on the Bath Road, was adapted and much extended to form a motel for the Watneys group. It has subsequently changed hands at least twice, and although it received a major refurbishment in 2000/2001,has been demolished

Before completing this survey, however, we must acknowledge that during the 19th Century a temperance movement sprang up, with some going for total abstinence from alcohol, and this prompted the establishment of Temperance Hotels. Frome had three significant such hotels, the Wallbridge Hotel (later renamed the Great Western Hotel), convenient for the railway station, and subsequently converted into the local tax offices; and Bull's Temperance Hotel in the Market Place (which ran a regular carriage service to the railway station), which was converted into the Post Office in 1913, and the Temperance Hotel designed by Joseph Chapman jr, which was demolished to form the Catherine Street car park. There were also a number of smaller establishments, two of those recorded being in Badcox (Pioneer) and Christchurch Street East (Minty's).

Having now looked at religious, public, industrial and commercial buildings, it is now time for us to turn our attention to the domestic buildings of Frome. These, like all the town's building types, very much reflect the social and commercial history of the town.

FOOTNOTES

1. Michael McGarvie: "The Book of Frome": Barracuda Books, 1980, and also other books by this author. This book reproduces the 1774 map of Frome as endpapers - much of the information in this chapter stems from this map.

2. Michael McGarvie: Op. cit.

3. Roger Leach and Derek Gill: "Early Industrial Housing - the Trinity Area of Frome: Royal Commission for Historic Monuments Supplementary Series No 3: HMSO, 1981

4. Michael McGarvie: Op. cit.

5. Derek Gill: "The Sheppards and Eighteenth Century Frome": Frome Society for Local Study, 1982

6. Derek Gill: Op. cit.

Further information comes from various Frome Almanacks and directories.

## THE PACK HORSE INN, CHRISTCHURCH STREET WEST

The terminal for the old colliers and their transport and set on Frome's
first "by-pass" between 1730 and 1750.

## CHURCH HOUSE,
## CHURCH STREET

First mentioned in 1300, it has
a pre-1600 timber frame.

THE DEVELOPMENT
OF FROME:
COMPARATIVE
MAPS, c 1650 TO 1985
All are to the same scale.

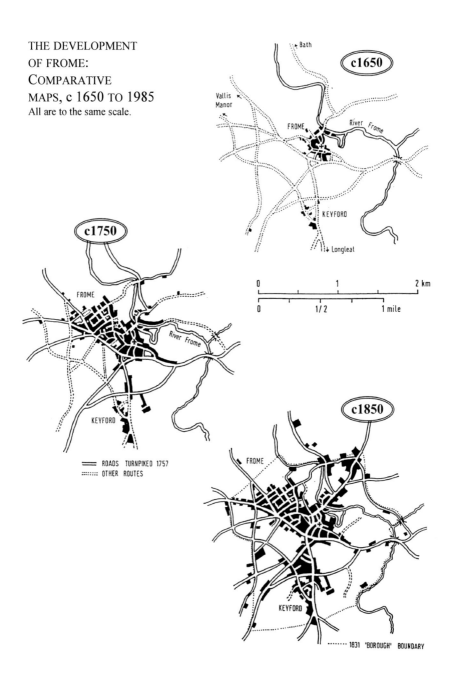

c1650

Bath

Vallis
Manor

FROME

River Frome

KEYFORD

Longleat

c1750

FROME

River Frome

KEYFORD

═══ ROADS TURNPIKED 1757
∷∷∷∷ OTHER ROUTES

c1850

FROME

KEYFORD

········ 1831 'BOROUGH' BOUNDARY

0          1          2 km

0        1/2       1 mile

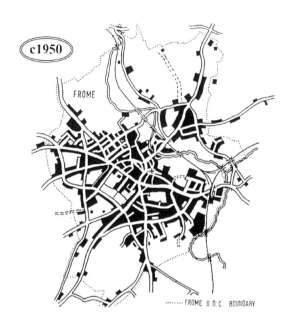

c1950

FROME

········ FROME U.D.C. BOUNDARY

c1985

FROME

FROME T.C. BOUNDARY
UP TO 1985 ········
AFTER 1985 ────

83

## Nos 27 AND 28 VICARAGE STREET

17th/18th Century houses embracing an early 16th Century archway, possibly connected with Frome's old tithe barn. (A R Yeates)

## GENTLE STREET

The Chantry and The Hermitage, two 16th Century or earlier houses, partially remodelled in the 18th Century.( G F J Russell)

# CHAPTER NINE
# PRE-1600 HOUSES IN FROME

It is not really surprising that there are very few pre-1600 houses in Frome or its near surroundings, as such buildings are relatively rare throughout the country. Most of the houses of such a time which still survive are either the very grand and well-built properties such as Longleat House, rebuilt after a serious fire in 1567 and more or less finished by 1580, (of which the owners, the Thynne family, possessed about one-third of the town of Frome until the 19th Century); or they were isolated farmhouses and yeoman's residences which did not come under the same pressure for redevelopment as did town houses. Houses built for ordinary people were not normally substantial enough to survive, and in any case they were far too small to cope with later standards of living, and so far more likely to be either demolished, or to be so altered as to become unrecognisable.

Apart from Longleat (which is outside the scope of this book, and adequately covered by other sources), by far the most important early house in the Frome District was Vallis Manor, the original home of the Lord of the Manor of Frome, and this too was just outside the town (above Egford: the word "vallis" is a corruption of the French word "falaise", meaning "cliff"). Much of the house survived into the 20th Century, and some records have been made of it, but it has now almost totally gone. We do not know when it was first built: the first written record is of Wandrille de Courcelles being allowed to have an oratory at his house from 1156 (acknowledging that the house was a fair distance from St John's Church). However, there is another reference to one Ralph Fitzbernard being allowed to build a lodge at Frome (almost certainly in Vallis) in 1235, and being permitted to cut down 10 oak trees in the king's forest for this purpose. The oak would have been principally for the roof frame, but there could well have been enough for a general timber frame as well. There was one pointed arch in the ruins of the manor building which in 1927 was considered to be of the 13th Century, but this has long since fallen down. The principal feature of the manor was the Great Hall, of which part of the roof structure survived until the 1970s: one expert dated it to about 1465, as it had arch-braced collar trusses and three ranks of arched wind-braces to the purlins. There were also several cambered-arched doorways and at least two 15th or 16th Century fireplaces. There were also attached extensions as well as outbuildings. Of the few fragments remaining, some were incorporated into a later farmhouse and cottages now on the site[1].

Another major early building was in the separate settlement of Keyford (which had its own entry in the 1086 Domesday Book, and which was not incorporated into Frome until the 19th Century): this was the residence of the Twynyhoe family, which may well have been the Manor House of Keyford. Sometimes known as The Old Nunnery, it was the home of a 16th Century nun Ankorette who suffered the indignity of being abducted and kidnapped by the Duke of Clarence for supposedly poisoning his wife, and despite her innocence she was subsequently hanged by him; he was later punished for this murder: this probably explains the name of the house - it was never an actual nunnery, but it is likely that Ankorette was connected with the Abbey of Shaftesbury. This property survives, in tantalising fragments, in the block of houses now known as 51-67 Lower Keyford. The thick walls here contain the remains of several door and window arches of the 13th and 14th Centuries, some of which are visible externally, and it is likely that more features are covered by plasterwork in the rooms of some of the present houses, which seemed to have developed with the division of the property taking place from the 17th Century onwards: some winder-staircases and stone fireplaces in these cottages are relics of this period. However, care is required in any works here: one lucky owner discovered some early 15th Century wall paintings when renovating his house in the 1970s, possibly associated with an altar - permission for a portable altar for the family here was granted by Pope Calixtus III in 1455[2].

The earliest fragments surviving in the Frome town centre could well be what remains of the Manor House of St Catherine, around the steps up into Sheppards Barton, embracing what is now Nos 13, 14 and 15 Catherine Hill. This property was first mentioned in 1253, and incorporated a chapel dedicated to St Catherine, as a "Chapel of Ease" to St John's Church. Again, a few fragments have been found, including parts of mediaeval roof trusses, some linenfold panelling; and the stones of two side windows said to have come from this property, and probably of 15th or 16th Century date, are now in Frome Museum. However, there could well be fragments elsewhere in the town awaiting discovery: many of Frome's stone houses were very well built, and the forest marble used for general walling is very durable, so that there was a tendency to alter properties rather than to rebuild them if at all possible. Even some "rebuilds" used the foundations and often considerable parts of earlier fabric.

Such fragments might be found in any of the properties in the early streets of the town: these include Church Slope (first mentioned in 1300); Vicarage Street, Twynhoestrete (now Gentle Street) and Cokkstrete (Eagle Lane), all mentioned in 1392; Cheap Street (1500 first mention) and the old Rook Lane and Stony Street (known by 1568). By implication, the Market Place may well have been the earliest site for houses, albeit with shops attached, the market being well established by 1086. What makes Frome fortunate in this respect is that most alterations to the central street pattern were fairly early, and most of what we have now, with the exception of Cork Street and Scott Road, had been established by 1830. There has been no later street widening: Frome was in depression during the most likely periods of "improvement", particularly in the Victorian era. Perhaps we should thank the far-sightedness of Thomas Bunn in his improvements forming North Parade and Bath Street, and reshaping of the Market Place, long before the motor vehicle was even dreamed of!

The Black Death, in the 14th Century, was instrumental in destroying or severely damaging many Somerset settlements (such as Cranmore, towards Shepton Mallet), but Frome seems to have escaped the worst - perhaps because of the abundant "nearly fresh" water which washed some of the town's streets, of which the Cheap Street stream is the last survivor. However, it is after this calamity that Frome's prosperity began to climb for some 400 years, although the ownership of the town by the Church until 1540, (the holdings of the Abbey of Cirencester, which had held Frome since 1150 or so, were bought out by the

Thynne family of Longleat around that time) may have somewhat inhibited its general development.. If we want to envisage pre-1600 Frome, Cheap Street (without the stone pavings) gives us the best idea. Most buildings would have had stone bases, but timber frames were common for the superstructure (and of course these were more vulnerable to fire or to later alteration).

I have already mentioned the properties of Cheap Street, which combined houses with shops at least as early as 1500, where most of the buildings are pre-1600 at least in part. Some other timber-framed buildings may be hidden by later stonework: Church House, on Church Steps, is a possibility: it is still partly timber framed above basement level, and has one timber mullioned window (now blocked) at the rear, as well as a splendid doorway, but it could be just after 1600. (Incidentally, the arch at basement level marks the place where the parish fire engine was stored until about the end of the 19th Century.) Not far away, in Vicarage Street, is the archway between Nos 27 and 28 Vicarage Street, which has been dated to around 1525. No 28 still has fragments of an earlier roof structure unrelated to the present property, but probably not as old as the archway. The adjacent walls of the houses do not relate to the archway, which could just possibly be part of the old bailiff's house which stood in this area. The whole of this side of the road was Church glebe land, and there was a great tithe barn further up the slope, probably where St John's School now stands. And does the Vicarage itself stand on old foundations? (I will be describing this more fully in a later chapter, as is more appropriate.)

One property (now divided) in Gentle Street is certainly pre-1600, and in its present form is known as The Chantry and The Hermitage. It is probably that referred to in 1548, when it was purchased separately by the Thynne family, and which became their Frome town house. In The Chantry what is claimed as a priest's hole was uncovered in 1958 (it is suggested that this might relate to the persecution of the Catholics by Edward VI (1547 to 1553 but in view of the general religious tolerance which seems to have prevailed in Frome it is perhaps unlikely)[3]. The property became known as Gentle Street House after James Wickham III (the solicitor, and builder of the present Blue House) purchased it in the early 18th Century (like several streets in Frome, including Castle Street, Horton Street, Button Street, Naish's Street etc., Gentle Street takes its current name from a former resident in the Street, one William Gentle). He remodelled it about 1740 or 1750, replacing the mullioned windows with then up-to-date sash windows (but leaving parts of the stone surrounds in position in the walls: despite recent repointing these can still be seen!), and reshaped some of the interior. Some of the details here are similar to St John's Vicarage, and I suspect that Nathaniel Ireson, the Wincanton architect, could have been involved here. Wickham certainly made his presence felt: he had some of the Twattle Alley properties below his house demolished, (leaving only those incorporated into the property next door), and also had the cottages opposite taken down (where the forecourt to the later Knoll House was), so that he had a clearer view of Rook Lane Chapel! A successor of his, who was much involved with the local militia, was presumably instrumental in getting the original Drill Hall next door constructed on what was part of his land (although the Wickhams moved into North Hill House, at the top of North Parade, in 1800)[4].

Another house which had a pre-1600 core was that nicknamed "Cockeys Manor", in Spring Road at Fromefield, which was demolished in the early 1970s to make way for the modern houses of Stoneleigh Rise. This was a long, low, rambling house which had apparently been remodelled early in the 18th Century. There are also some indications that the Old Presbytery, at West End, may incorporate some fragments of the late 15th or early 16th Century. This property has sometimes been identified with the Manor of St Catherine, although the Catherine Hill/ Sheppards Barton site is the more likely. Indirect evidence suggests that it had a dovecote, and the Conigar, its correct location, implies a rabbit-warren (where rabbits were bred for food). A part of an early moulded window- head of this period still survives, but the small lancet windows (which would normally suggest a 13th or early 14th Century date), are in fact of the 19th Century.

I am unable to ascribe a pre-1600 date to any other remaining houses in Frome on exposed architectural evidence, but I would not rule out the possibility of discovering one or two more in the course of time. However, after 1600 we find a substantial number of houses, of all sizes, being built in the town, culminating in the Newtown, or Trinity Area development of 1665 to 1725, which in its scale was not to be matched until the post-1950 development of the town, and we will deal with these in the next two chapters.

FOOTNOTES

1. Michael McGarvie: "The Book of Frome": Barracuda Books, 1980

2. Francis Kelly (investigator for) the Statutory List of Buildings of Architectural or Historic Importance in Frome, and also the Frome Society for Local Study Year Book 6, p78 where James White, the then owner of the house, writes of the works carried out here in 1980-81, and of the discoveries made in the house.

3. Peter Belham: "The Making of Frome": Frome Society for Local Study, 1973

4. Michael McGarvie: Op. cit.

# CHAPTER TEN

## SEVENTEENTH CENTURY FROME HOUSES, EXCLUDING THE TRINITY AREA

In 1607 it is recorded that Robert Smith, of a family of clothiers, purchased a site for his house: unfortunately we know little more of him personally, but we do know that his family owned two major 17th Century Frome houses. Rook Lane House, and what is now known as Stonewall Manor, Lower Keyford (actually approached from Culverhill). It would seem reasonable to suppose that one of these two houses was built on the site referred to, but I would consider the Rook Lane House to be the more likely, especially in the light of a datestone at Stonewall Manor which I shall discuss later. Rook Lane House has been much altered over the years, not least by the addition of a Gothic style bay window which was added in the late 19th Century (just possibly salvaged from somewhere else), but the relieving arches which can be clearly seen over a number of the windows are typical of a number of 17th Century Frome buildings: however only the attic windows are likely to be originals. The doorcase is of the late 18th Century, but the interior is largely of the 19th Century. The house is noted for one of its sometime residents, the poetess Elizabeth Rowe, who numbered amongst her friends Bishop Ken, and Isaac Watts the hymn writer.

The other Smith house, Stonewall Manor, was for many years known as the Austin's House. This is thought to be not a reference to a previous owner, but a misinterpretation of local tradition which averred that there was a priory at Keyford, and this was the most likely site. In fact, as described in the previous chapter, the religious title, if deserved, should belong to the properties opposite, Nos 51-67 Lower Keyford[1]. This house, despite what must have been a substantial restoration of c1900, is one of the best of Frome's 17th Century houses (if you accept the fact that Keyford is now part of Frome!), and gives us a very good idea of what the grander house of the period was like. In general character it is like many of the Cotswold houses, and Frome houses of the time had a great affinity with that area, (which, like Frome, was a prime wool-producing area), to such an extent that Frome might almost be considered to mark the southernmost extent of the Cotswolds. Its three-gabled principal elevation has a central door with a 1683 datestone set over the lintel, but I am inclined to think that this date relates to a family event (such as a wedding), or a remodelling of the house at that time, because there are two fireplaces of distinctly Tudor character, a fine staircase and a decorated plasterwork ceiling which are certainly more of the earlier 17th Century in character. (As with many houses of this era, the staircase is in a separate turret to the rear, an arrangement found in a number of other houses in the town, including Nos 16-17 Stony Street, No 3 Cork Street, some Trinity Area houses and one or two in the oldest parts of The Butts.)

No 26 Vicarage Street is a fine town house which is almost certainly of the first quarter of the 17th Century. It was built on church glebe land, and the Vicar (living opposite until recently) still has some rights of consultation over any works carried out to the house! There is some mystery about this house: the formal elevation is that to Vicarage Street, but works carried out to the house in the 1970s showed that the then current front door was a 19th Century insertion, whilst there was an old glazed fanlight and door to the rear- perhaps the archway between Nos 27 and 28 may give a clue, as indeed may the house on the corner of Vicarage Street and Blindhouse Lane, where the front door was in the angle opposite the Blindhouse Lane front: the foundations of possible former houses which occur half-way up the garden of No 28 also suggest that there was probably some different street layout, or perhaps a barton, here at one time. (The 1774 map, which is somewhat sketchy, does not show this latter house, but there is a considerable widening of Vicarage Street shown at this point). To get back to No 26, however: it has a fine, wide curving stair with moulded risers set in a separate turret, and a painted skirting to the stairs uncovered during the works, has been dated stylistically to between 1610 and 1620. The kitchen was in a low two-storey rear extension, with a former well set in the floor. One of the most striking features, however, is the fireplace to the main ground floor room, which bears a datestone of 1683 in the fireback. Closer examination shows that the chimney breast is straight- jointed with the main walls, and so is almost certainly a later addition. Some six or seven of these datestones survive in the older parts of Frome, and it would seem that some stonemason was hard at work installing proper fireplaces with flues in Frome houses between about 1680 and 1685 (one has already been mentioned in the former Angel and Crown Inn in Vallis Way, and others have been found at 13 Bath Street, 1 Trinity Street, a house at Fromefield - undefined, it may have been "Cockeys Manor" - as well as one or two Trinity Area houses, where the date is more likely to be the actual construction date of the house rather than of an insertion).

Perhaps it is worth a short digression here: smaller earlier houses would only have had a hearth (not necessarily a fireplace) where food was to be cooked, and these were often only in a single-storey building or part of a building, (two-storey cottages are common only from the early 17th Century onwards: earlier cottages have often had a floor inserted later, hence the low ceilings) and the smoke was just allowed to go up through the roof, normally through a vent formed for the purpose: this is why so many old houses have smoke- blackened rafters. Some two-storey cottages had fireplaces with flues, but certainly in South Somerset (where a few still survive), the flue was timber-framed and plastered with cow-dung, which is relatively fire-resisting. Of course there was a fire risk, especially if the roof was thatched, but the fact that some still survive after 400 years shows that they were not so risk prone as one might imagine. Most fires were of timber logs (coal was only widely used as a fuel as water and then rail transport became available), but of course Frome was near enough to the mines of Mells and Radstock to allow it to be brought in by pack horse, so coal was available relatively early to those who could afford it), and by the end of the 18th Century there was a serious timber shortage in the country, and much had to be imported from the Baltic and also Canada. With coal, it was more important to have proper flues because of the fumes generated by its burning. Obviously it was the Frome fashion to have a proper fireplace and flue inserted in the 1680s!

Another 17th Century house was nearby in Merchants Barton (which was a continuation of Church Street into what is now the Notts Industries factory yard): unfortunately it was demolished about 1970 to make way for Saxon Vale. I did see it before it went: indeed I was offered the building as an office by the old Urban District Council, but this was beyond the reach of a young architect just starting out in practice, and sadly I had to decline - if only.... ! The main façade had a large single gable, with deep transomed windows at first floor level, somewhat reminiscent of the Longleat pattern. This house was the home of the Merchant Family (the word "barton" is often used locally to denote a cluster of buildings, usually houses, all belonging to a single family) and the family initials and the date 1650 appeared in a first floor ceiling in very elaborate moulded plaster. This ceiling was saved when the building was demolished, and now graces the flat attached to The Barn in Bradford on Avon, (not the tithe barn), the headquarters of the Bradford on Avon Preservation Trust. The ground floor had vine leaf- decorated timber beams which were going to be put into store, but I have not seen them since. (Right up to 1970 Frome lost a number of important historic buildings, which should have been spot-listed and saved: this had two consequences, one was the formation of the Frome and District Civic Society - now merged with the Frome Society for Local Study - and the other was an emergency re-listing of Frome's historic buildings by the government, as the risk to Frome's historical treasures became publicised nation-wide)[2].

Another house which might well have suffered the same fate, and which is also of a c1650 date, is Nos 3/3B Cork Street, fortunately carefully restored a few years ago. This had some considerable 18th and 19th Century alterations, especially in the attic, which led to a complicated roof pattern, and the subsequent ingress of water which caused much damage. Again, this had deep transomed mullioned windows at first floor level, the labels surviving over ground floor widows despite the insertion of later shopfronts. Originally there were three or possibly four attic gables before the alterations. Again, there is a fine first floor plaster ceiling of rather similar character to that at Merchants Barton, but with more elaborate vine scrolling, and a shield and griffin frieze. According to local tradition (and reiterated on the 1774 map of Frome), this is the house where the Duke of Monmouth stayed on the nights of 18 th and 29th June 1685 at the height of the Rebellion, (and where he would have made the fateful decision not to proceed to Warminster to do battle with the King's forces, but to retreat to Glastonbury where he had been promised greater support, from where he was forced to do battle on Sedgemoor with inferior troops, with the result that the Rebellion was crushed). Monmouth had much support in Frome, and one can imagine that a newish house in the very centre of the town was deemed most appropriate for him, whereas his officers could stay at the nearby inns. (Monmouth House, next door, perpetuates this tradition, but the house itself was built some time after 1685)[3]. Just across the road was Hall House, a substantial house first recorded in 1635, but probably rebuilt or remodelled later in the 17th Century. It was demolished in 1935.

Just above the church, in what was then Rook Lane, is a terrace of houses which we know now as 11-15 Bath Street. (No 10, at the top, is believed to be a rebuild of 1760 or soon after). These were on Longleat lands, and some leases survive which assist in their dating: No 12 goes back at least to 1665, No 13 is before 1686 (it has a dated "Frome fireplace" of 1683), and No 15 to 1654: the other two only have later leases. However, these are arch-typical 17th Century Frome houses, whose pattern was to be repeated frequently in the Trinity Area from 1665 onwards. They have timber casement windows (these might have been stone mullioned originally) and the attic gables which occur so frequently in the town. Originally their front doors opened directly on to the street, but whereas the houses opposite were destroyed to make way for the new Bath Street, this group of houses gained considerable front gardens!

Similar smaller houses are to be found in Keyford, at Nos 5 and 6 (originally one larger house): these, with the Crown Inn, suggest that the process of joining the hamlet of Keyford to Frome probably began in the 17th Century. Some original details survive here. Another similar pair of houses is at Nos 7 and 8 Gentle Street, which have the mullioned windows and gables, winder stairs with moulded risers, and various beams and doorways of the 17th Century. No 4 Gentle Street is also of this period. In King Street, No 18 and the houses adjoining it in Church Street, are more of the same, although No 18 has Tudor rose decoration to the ceiling plasterwork, and a very early fireplace, which might suggest a core before 1600. No 1 Church Street has an early 19th Century façade planted on, and No 3, which has some timber framing, might also be earlier than 1600. Other similar houses are to be found at Nos 4 and 5 Catherine Street (although No 4 may also be pre-1600), and a group of cottages in Keyford, Nos 30, 32, 40, 44 and 47. Some houses in Whittox Lane and Sun Street could also be pre-1700 in origin.

Going back to larger houses, there is Melrose House in Whittox Lane, originally with transomed windows like Merchants Barton, but remodelled in the 18th Century. Some of the original side and rear windows have been blocked, almost certainly as a result of the Window Tax, introduced in 1697 when William III was short of funds: the house must have been almost lantern-like and very light inside when first built. The main façade seems to have been remodelled about 1740, and most of the internal features, including a splendid staircase, are of this later period. In the principal ground and first floor rooms, the blocked windows were covered with fielded panelling, on which some rather fine 18th Century views were painted (a very "18th Century thing" of which all too few examples now survive - there are some in Bath, and one or two south of Bruton: these were too obscured by varnish to be readily identified, and needed specialist cleaning when I last saw them).

Another major house with 17th Century origins, but which had a mid-18th Century make-over, is The Iron Gates in King Street, now the pet stores. Only the rear elevations and basement were unaltered, because the interior was totally reshaped as its owners, the Sheppards (the major clothiers in Frome), prospered in their business. The house really has to be read as a very fine Georgian house now. Another house of pre-1700 is Westbrook House (No 33 Vicarage Street, on the corner of Blindhouse Lane). This may only just come into the 17th Century: its detailing is rather similar to some of the houses on the south-west side of Vallis Way (which I shall be covering in the next chapter, one of which was dated 1697). As we have already seen with No 26, there has been some change in the street pattern here, with the result that the principal entrance is in the internal angle of the L-plan building. It probably related to Twattle Alley, which ran along the southern edge of St John's churchyard. This has mullioned and transomed windows, and the original door under a cornice hood. The Blindhouse Lane elevation features an oculus (oval window), a detail which is also found in Vallis Way, and several windows which appear to have been blocked when the Window Tax was introduced. This house was used as a school in the 19th Century, and later became a shop.

On the whole this is not a bad collection of 17th Century houses for a small town, but in the next chapter we look at the Trinity Area of the town, which features many more, mostly small, houses which were erected in the second half of the 17th and the first quarter of the 18th Centuries. This is now seen as a national treasure, and has been acknowledged as such after nearly being destroyed.

FOOTNOTES

1.  Michael McGarvie: "The Book of Frome", Barracuda Books, 1980: the tale of the nun is recounted in Michael's "Frome Through The Ages": Frome Society for Local Study, 1982.

2.  Colin Amery and Dan Cruikshank: "The Rape of Britain": Paul Elek, 1975, devoted a whole chapter on Frome, one of thirty cities and towns in Britain which the authors selected to illustrate how much of Britain's history was demolished in the early years after the Second World War.

3.  Robert Dunning: "The Monmouth Rebellion": Dovecote Press, 1984.

The author has visited most of the houses described in this chapter over the years, and indeed was employed professionally to oversee the restoration or updating of a few. As an aide memoire the descriptions given in the Statutory List for Frome were also consulted.

## STONEWALL MANOR, LOWER KEYFORD
Dated 1683, the style so traditional it suggests the reuse of earlier fabric.

## KEYFORD
Some of the 16th, 17th and 18th Century houses which formed part of the separate village of Keyford, "swallowed up" by Frome by the mid-19th Century. (A R Yeates)

## COURT HOUSE AND IRON GATES, KING STREET

Iron Gates was built before 1696; Court House was added possibly c1710, and both were modified c1760: both belonged to the Sheppard family.

## WINE STREET HOUSE

The front is of c1740, to fit the new street, but behind is a fabric at least 100 years older.

# CHAPTER ELEVEN
# THE DEVELOPMENT OF THE TRINITY AREA 1665 - 1725

It is salutary to think that in 1973, after interminable debate, what remains of Frome's Trinity Area, excluding the north side of Trinity Street, (which had been radically restored by the Frame Urban District Council), remained under a Slum Clearance Order, despite growing local opposition. The first sector of this "Newtown", between Trinity Street and Milk Street (to the north of the old Selwood Printing Works) was demolished in 1960, and replaced by houses and flats designed by Vallis and Vallis of Frome (the flats have since been demolished and replaced with new housing). Then in 1963-64 most of the next area, below Trinity Street and on the other side of Selwood Road/ Welshmill Lane, was cleared and redeveloped to designs by the municipal engineer, C H Lewis, on a layout put forward by the then Ministry of Housing and Local Government; only the north side of Trinity Street being saved, so as to preserve the aspect of Trinity Church. (These few houses were linked to a district heating scheme serving the new houses, which proved to be a failure). Up to this time, no one had really investigated the history of the area, which was generally thought to be of the 19th Century, albeit in the rather conservative style which might have survived in a small country town, and the time-relationship of the houses to Holy Trinity Church was not considered. The houses were small and sites were cramped and generally insanitary, and most were leasehold. Of the few that were privately owned, compulsory purchase was invoked, and site values only were paid - sometimes as little as £6 or £8 per house. All was set for the next phase of redevelopment, which would have seen the destruction of the remainder of the area, despite the efforts of the newly formed Frome and District Civic Society, and also the Save Trinity Group, which consisted mostly of local residents who cared about the area. Just at the crucial moment however, the 1974 local government reorganisation took place, and the plans were deferred.

As Lord Adeane said in his foreword to the published study of the Trinity Area by The Royal Commission on Historical Monuments:

"Only then was it realised that many of the houses formed part of an extensive urban development of the late 17th Century. Preliminary research indicated that few, if any, urban estates of this period survived elsewhere, comparable examples in towns such as London and Manchester having been replaced by later development. Moreover, the first full-scale study recently published of 18th Century urban building in England had emphasised the lack of evidence about houses, and especially the smaller ones, of the early 18th Century".

But despite the demolitions already carried out, Frome had some 137 houses of this era which the Royal Commission, in conjunction with the Committee for Rescue Archaeology in Avon, Gloucestershire and Somerset, was able to survey. I was privileged to be involved with this survey in a very small way, but I would not presume to match the excellent report entitled "Early Industrial Housing" which was published by the RCHM as a result of that survey, and I would strongly commend it to anyone who wishes to study the area in greater detail. All of the subsequent material in this chapter relies heavily on this report, and in particular on the information provided by Roger Leach and Derek Gill.

The church rate books show that between 1660 and 1695 the number of Frome's rateable inhabitants quadrupled - such was the population explosion of this period. As a result, Frome was then thought to be bigger than Bath and possibly larger than Salisbury. Almost all of this growth took place in the Newtown (or the Trinity Area as it became known after Holy Trinity Church was erected to serve the area in 1837-38). In 1665 there were just a few houses along the north-east side of Vallis Way, and shortly afterwards Long Row (later Castle Street, after a Mrs Castle who lived in the large house at the end of the street) was developed. By 1684 other roads were appearing, including Milk Street and Cross Street/ Nail Street (now the eastern end of Trinity Street), then Milking Barton (York Street), and Long Street (which became Selwood Road in 1901, possibly at the same time as it was extended into Vallis Way, having previously terminated at Baker Street). By 1705 The Ope, Naish's Street and the south-western side of Vallis Way had been developed; Long Street had been extended by Broad Street (replaced by a realigned Selwood Road in the 1960s) so that it met Milk Street; and a loop called Bell Lane had also been formed. By 1725 Trooper Street (the western end of Trinity Street), Duke Street, Peter Street, The Mint and Dyers Close Lane were built (these last being the area that was cleared in the 1960s), and the Newtown was virtually complete.

The street layout was more or less on a grid pattern, albeit adapted to fit the old field boundaries, of which at least five fields of differing ownership were involved. The street widths were determined in multiples of five feet (1.6m). Trooper Street, which became the focus of a new market, was 35 feet (11m), then came Naish's Street at 30 feet (nearly 10 m), and the narrowest were mere back alleys of 15 feet (5m) and 10 feet width (such as York Street and Duke Street). It is perhaps significant that it was the later houses that were demolished first under the slum clearance orders - presumably these tended to be smaller and closer together, as more people, with less money available, clamoured to move into the new area.

The method of the development of the area has proved to be of great significance, because the three principal landowners who promoted this exercise leased the plots rather than selling them outright: interestingly, until the history of the Trinity Area came to light, it was thought that the principle of leasehold development had originated in Bristol in about 1710. The principle was not entirely new - development on manorial and church lands had been carried out in this fashion for years, but only on a single-house basis, not for multiple properties and occupation. Basically, plots of land mostly between 13 and 18 feet wide (4m to 5.5m), and between 100 and 150 feet (30m to 45m) long, were leased out for one year to an intending builder, during which time the house had to be built. The lease was then renegotiated and a lease given for 99 years, or three "lives" if this proved to be the shorter time, after which ownership of the whole property as well as the plot would revert to the family of the original owner. (The system of "lives" produced an extra income for the landowner: in the agreement three people - normally younger members of the lessee's family - would be named, and the property would stay with the lessee as long as these lived: on the death of the last of the three named the lease could be renegotiated, for a fee payable to the landowner, for the balance of the 99 years). Up to about 1750 the yearly rents varied between two and three shillings. This 99 year lease period was significant in the architectural history of the area: the area tended to become run down as the leases expired, and there would be a flurry of remodelling as new 99 year leases were made. By 1960 the leases were about to expire for the third time, and although some properties had been bought outright by their occupants the majority were still leasehold (with a few mostly absentee landlords), making the assembly of the area as a landholding by the local authority a relatively easy matter.

The waves of deterioration and restoration are fairly easy to spot in the buildings of the area: in a few cases buildings were totally rebuilt; in others a new façade was planted on; in others an extra storey was added, or the roof reformed. Rarely were plots altered, except where some houses had another built at the bottom of their garden, an alleyway or ginnel being carved out of the original house (bearing in mind that all of these houses were in continuous terraces) for access. Some examples of this "back-garden" development could be found to two houses in Naish's Street, and also in Selwood Road and Vallis Way. One absentee landlord was advised at the beginning of the 19th Century that so many houses in the area were ruinous or empty that there was no chance of increasing the rents! The Slum Clearance Order, then, after some of the houses had had almost 300 years of life, was therefore perhaps no surprise. However, in the light of the RCHM Report, the Slum Clearance Order was unwound (possibly for the first and only time), and instead the area was designated as both an Outstanding Conservation Area and as a General Improvement Area.

Acting on the advice of the Royal Institute of British Architects, the new Mendip District Council commissioned a report from the architectural practice of Moxley, Jenner and Partners of Bristol (who had at that time just completed a very successful restoration of the Christmas Steps area in Bristol), and subsequently they were employed to supervise the rehabilitation of the whole area (that is, of the properties owned by Mendip District Council). The works started in 1980 and were completed in 1984, after some £4 million had been spent on the project. As had been the case with the previous two periods when leases had expired, some houses were demolished (mostly unsuitable 19th Century houses, including Nos 4 to 6 Trinity Street, a most unsightly brick terrace which looked very "out of place"), some were amended, some knocked two-into-one, and all overhauled and brought up to modern standards. One or two new houses of sympathetic design were added. Despite this, (and the fact that some houses had been damaged by squatters and looters during the period when the houses were empty) there are still many original features surviving in the houses. Some of the gardens were shortened to enable the formation of joint parking areas, so that the narrow roads would not be blocked with cars. The road pattern was adjusted slightly, and a few trees (surely the first in the area for 300 years!) were planted. Some of the original proposals were not adopted, but more detailed information on individual properties may be found both in the 1978 Report, and in the Commemorative Brochure published by Mendip District Council in 1984. The final result was the achievement of a Housing Award for both the Council and their architects.

So who lived in these houses when they were first built? This is not an easy question to answer, as it was not always the builder who lived in the houses - some were rented out. It is easy to say that most of the residents were woollen workers employed by the Sheppards at Spring Gardens - doubtless many were (judging from the number of footpaths across the fields from the Trinity Area to Spring Gardens), but of the known occupations of those building the last phase, seven were masons, at least three were cardmakers, four were carpenters, one was a tiler and another a handstock maker. Several people built more than one house: Thomas Lacey, a carpenter built six in the area between 1719 and 1724; Thomas Coombs and William Coombes, both masons, built two apiece, and other members of both the Lacey and Coombs families built houses too. Some were presumably built as speculation and investment, but others were built for other members of the same family, which might help to explain the remarkable community spirit which existed in the area right up to 1972, when the last occupants were moved out and resettled in The Mount, on the other side of Frome. (The social effects of this wholesale resettlement were enormous, and perhaps never fully appreciated by those concerned: I well remember one couple in their nineties who did not wish to move - one had lived there the whole of her life: her husband had been there for 70 years. Another old lady was used to just a single water tap in her kitchen, and had no gas or electricity - she was really worried as to how she could cook without her paraffin stove, and how she would adjust to having hot water, electricity and central heating. Another old man was worried as to how he would fare alone: in Trinity if he failed to take in his milk, or draw his curtains back by a certain time, Mrs So-and-so who lived opposite would knock on his door to see if he was all right - how could anyone see him on the new estate, where the houses were so far apart?.)

An analysis is made in the RCHM Report of the character of the original house types, and well over half were of the same simple design; two or three storeys of one room only on each floor. On one party wall would be the big open fireplace, which was used for cooking, keeping the precious salt dry (usually on a special shelf or in a little cupboard next to the flue), and heating the whole house - the fire would never go out. Alongside the flue would be the staircase, usually of a winding, semi-circular pattern: the front wall would have a mullioned window of two, three or even four lights width, according to the width of the house: the depth of the house was fairly constant at 13 feet (4m). The front door, on the corner furthest from the fireplace, would lead straight from the street into the living/ cooking space; opposite, in the back wall would be another door, with another window, under which might be some form of sink. Upstairs the rooms would be plain, usually without another fireplace - in winter all would huddle around the flue for warmth. Furniture would be minimal: the all-important settle between the front wall and the window would help to keep the worst of the draughts away from those privileged to sit there, otherwise there might be a table and a few stools, and possibly even a storage chest. Upstairs there might be a storage cupboard or perhaps just a few pegs on the wall (if the family was rich enough to possess a change of clothes or bedlinen), but the beds would most likely be straw palliasses. The staircase would probably have doors to it at each level; but one house seen had only a three-quarter height partition, rather typical of the 18th Century, and this same house (one of the least altered until 1972) had a part-glazed partition around the sink - probably more than most had. Toilet facilities were the closet at the bottom of the garden. One or two houses had fancy panelling, probably a later addition; but the odds were that these were the houses of carpenters and joiners anyway, who wanted their house to look as good as the houses they were accustomed to building for other people! We tend to forget how simply people lived in the 18th Century: what is more, some families amounted to 10 or 12 persons in one small house!

Of course, over a period of time the cottages were extended, most of them having a two-room extension at the rear with a small kitchen and a second bedroom over, and by the end of the 19th Century most would have a water closet closer to the house than the

99

old privy. Another fairly common modification was the addition of another storey in place of the attic gables: Nos 40 to 43 Naish's Street show this rather clearly: the upper stonework is of a somewhat different character. Sometimes the roof was lifted just a foot or two to give extra headroom in the attic: a slightly later house on the edge of the Trinity Area, on the corner of Horton Street, displays an end gable with three different roof lines. The terraces appear to have had a certain degree of uniformity at first; the uniform depth meant that after the first house had been built in each row, only three walls were needed to enclose each subsequent house. The streets were fairly level, which meant that the roof line could be continuous, punctuated by the gable which was a feature of all but the meanest houses. It is instructive to look at the streets now and to trace all the changes over a 300 year period: this exercise is developed in the RCHM book, with several sets of street elevations and a number of interesting photographs.

Scattered about in this grid layout were several larger houses, for the most part unexplained, except that they may have pre-dated the Newtown development. No 45 Milk Street, which appears to be late 17th Century, was Lewis Cockey's "bell house": its façade is of the late 18th Century, which may reflect its subsequent conversion into a public house, the Star and Garter. Similarly Nos 62/63 Naish's Street were once a single property, also a public house, the Dolphin Inn. No 1 Trinity Street, as we have already seen, was the King's Head Inn, and the toll collection point for those taking goods into central Frome. No 7 was also larger than most, and detached: it dates from c1680, and is of particular interest because of its fine brick-lined cellar (with underground tunnels leading from it which were said to go for a considerable distance - brickwork is rare at this date in Frome), and an elaborate newelled staircase. It had a three-room ground floor plan, including a large kitchen at the rear. The neighbouring property, No 8, was the Bell Inn, of three storeys with a late 18th Century façade. Another row of larger houses is to be found in Vallis Way, where Nos 4 to 9 were built at the end of the 17th Century. No 4, Byrlton House, was given a new façade in the 19th Century, but No 5, which bears a replacement datestone of 1697 with the motto "Time trieth troth" (now the motto on the town's armorial bearings), has cruciform windows similar to those of Melrose House. It can be seen that Nos 6, 7, and 8 were similar, but the mullions and transomes were cut out and replaced by sash windows in the 19th Century. There were oculi (oval windows) to the staircases, and the standard of provision for each house was more generous than those of the houses in the opposite streets, all having three rooms per floor. These houses were restored privately in the 1980s, under the guidance of the Frome Historic Buildings Trust Ltd.

The impact of this development on Frome must have been tremendous, but 1725 did not mark the end of small-house development in the town; it was rather more a slowing-down, with smaller pockets of development on a less planned basis. In the next chapter we shall see how the Trinity area not only became absorbed into the old town, but was itself extended.

FOOTNOTE
I can only reiterate that the prime source for the study of the Trinity Area (as we now know it) has to be the Royal Commission on Historical Monuments Supplementary Series No 3: "Early Industrial Housing: The Trinity Area of Frome", HMSO 1981, although strictly speaking, these were not industrial houses in the sense that would come to be applied in the 19th Century.

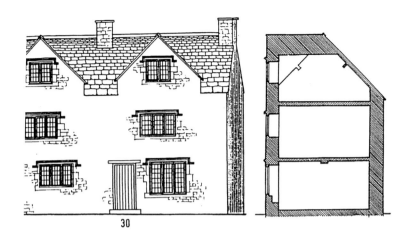

30

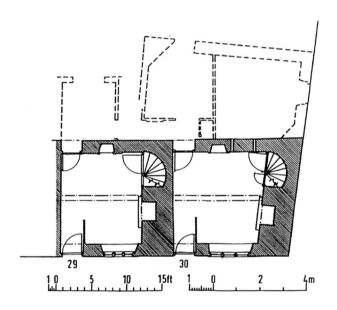

29                30

1 0     5     10    15ft   1   0       2       4m

## TYPICAL TRINITY AREA HOUSES,
## CONJECTURED ORIGINAL FORM
Based on surveys carried out by the author for the
Frome Rescue Archaeology Group in the 1970s.

101

## TRINITY AREA AS RESTORED: TRINITY STREET

The old King's Head Inn was on the corner, opposite the later Selwood Printing works: these houses were all in Cross Street (now part of Trinity Street).

## TRINITY AREA AS RESTORED: THE OPE

A cul de sac built about 1690, but with modifications of several dates since then. (A R Yeates)

# CHAPTER TWELVE
# FROME HOUSES OF THE EARLIER EIGHTEENTH CENTURY

By about 1700 Frome was really a boom town, and there was considerable building activity not only in the Newtown or Trinity Area, but around the periphery of the old town, and even some rebuilding or considerable remodelling in the old town itself. The total number of houses for the working class population was increasing rapidly as greater wealth was being created in the town, particularly through the manufacture of woollen cloth, and it is not surprising that the mill owners and merchants were also seeking higher standards of living in new houses. The Newtown had been virtually detached from Frome at the outset, with only tenuous links via a footpath from what we know now as Cork Street up to Matthews Barton (of which Sun Street was a part); by various footpaths off Catherine Hill and Badcox Lane (Catherine Street) and from Badcox, which was really the only point where old met new. It is not surprising, therefore, that a considerable proportion of the early 18th Century development should be in the nature of infill between the old and new towns - but of course such development could only take place where the appropriate landowners were willing. As it happens, the Sheppards were one of the landowners involved, and they were quite happy to see some of their land developed (possibly because by this time their principal houses were in Angel Lane/King Street, whereas they had formerly had No 13 to 15 Catherine Hill as their main residence), and it was probably with development in mind that William Sheppard had bought the land on which High Street now stands.

Even Catherine Street was not fully developed until the Newtown had arrived, but the top end, towards Badcox, was being developed soon after 1730, which was the time when, on the Sheppards' lands, the construction of High Street and Wine Street was begun (even though Wine Street House had existed in part 100 years earlier). Interestingly, it had been the churches which were built first - the Quaker Meeting House in 1675, and the Baptist Chapel next door in 1708 - both located on Sheppards Lane, which led out of the Barton from 13 Catherine Hill and along the edge of the Sheppards' land, (which later became South Parade); the Badcox Lane Baptist Chapel followed in 1712, and Nos 2 and 3 Sheppards Barton are certainly of early 18th Century date[1]. Behind this last chapel Catherine Hill House (No 3 Catherine Street) had been built only a short time earlier (it is first recorded in 1712), for the Whitchurch family.. This is a fine 5-bay two storey early Georgian style house with a stone pediment surround to the front door (the main façade being at right angles to Catherine Street); on the south side is a later two-storey bay window (possibly dating from soon after it changed hands in 1805)[2]. Sadly, the Frome Urban District Council, and their successors Mendip District Council, owned the premises from 1962 to 1982, during which time some problem families were housed there and much damage was done to the panelled interior: the house is now back in private ownership and has been remodelled. It is possible that this house sits on mediaeval foundations, on account of a tunnel discovered underneath the house, and indeed there is a local tradition of a house here having been burnt down in the 17th Century.

As had been the case with the Trinity Area, the houses in Wine Street and High Street were leasehold developments; few details exist of the individual houses, but all save Nos 1 and 2 Wine Street (which were built in the garden of No 16 Christchurch Street West in the early 19th Century) and Nos 3 and 4 (built in the garden of No 6, also in the 19th Century), were built by the time William Sheppard died in 1755. Most tend to be rather simpler than the Trinity houses elevationally, without the attic gables, but they are two small rooms deep. By this time, Behind Town (now Christchurch Street West) was taking shape, and it was to become a full toll road in 1757. The Pack Horse Inn was of about 1740, and some of the other properties between Badcox and South Parade must have their origins, at least, in the first half of the 18th Century. The other main link between the old and new towns, Whittox Lane, seems to have come later: one major house there, No 10 dates from 1754, according to its deeds (although there is a possibility that there was a house here earlier, and that this later date signifies a remodelling since the house has a 1693 datestone). Matthews Barton (Sun Street) may have been developed in the late 1600s (No 13 Sun Street has a 1690 datestone), and from the orientation of Melrose House (see Chapter 10) may well have formed the main route from the Newtown into the old town centre, although the 1774 map shows what is now Zion Path as a water course leading to the River Frome.

The Newtown area continued to attract further development in the first half of the 18th Century, and Vallis Way was extended, with Horton Street, Button Street, and Union Street (also known as Starve Acre, now supplanted by the Vallis Way/Dorset Close housing) being developed around this time. Included in the Trinity Area was the remarkable Castle Street House (now known as "The Keep" which ironically perpetuates the myth of an earlier building here, rather than the fact that "Castle" was a family name), and which remains a bit of an enigma: why build a grander house here in the middle of so many smaller houses, and why use a brick façade - it may well have been the only brick façade in Frome for nearly 150 years! There also seems to have been some construction of isolated houses and groups of cottages "out in the country", for we begin to find single houses of this time in Broadway and The Butts (where No 44 is dated 1700), and there are two interesting groups at Mount Pleasant, Nos 3-5, 8-12, and also Nos 8,9,11 and 11A Little Keyford; and also in Keyford is Keyford Farmhouse, with early 18th Century origins, at least, and also the group known as "New Buildings", which was recorded by 1730. Not surprisingly, the links along the road to Keyford were further strengthened with new houses, and also a public house (the Unicorn, which stood where the fire station is now, and was of early to mid-18th Century date). A few houses in Christchurch Street East (Behind Town) could well be of pre-1750 origins, as may be those in Plumbers and Clavey's Bartons (the latter shown as Vicarage Street Hill on the 1886 map).

Back towards the old town centre, the Sheppards were actively remodelling their houses in Angel Lane, The Iron Gates and Court House, both conveniently close to their Town Mills. The former is just pre-1700, as we have seen, but it was soon followed by Court House (which was never used for legal purposes, unless the occasional informal legal business was done there by Jack and William Sheppard, who were both magistrates)[3]. The slightly severe elevation of Court House, probably remodelled between 1740 and 1750, is relieved by a beautiful timber shell hood over the entrance door (although from its condition and design it could well be a good replacement of the early 1900s). This is echoed by a group of three houses in Willow Vale, Nos 14 to 16, which have similar door hoods, this time in stone, which date from around 1720; these are also imposing by their severity. Nearby, Willow Vale House, with a columned portico, was erected before 1741, although this had a remodelling about 1816. It was extended by the addition of The Willows at the same time, by John Olive, one of the family of dyers - showing that at that time most major employers still liked to live close to their manufacturing premises. At the beginning of Willow Vale, Nos 1 and 2, very much more modest, seem to date from this era, and may have been the first smaller houses on this side of the river.

Back in the Market Place, in 1719 Wilkins the Salter built another fine 5-bay early Georgian style house on the site of what is now the corner formed by Scott Road and The Bridge, which must have rivalled the 1688 house at No 17 Stony Street. This was built at right angles to the Market Place, and effectively blocked off the northern end visually: it features on many postcard views up until the time of its demolition in 1938. On the other side of the bridge, really marking the spread of the town on the other side of the river for the first time, was Bridge House, and next door the Black Swan Inn. Bridge House, for many years the offices of legal firms, retains much of its original detail, although there was some Regency period remodelling: I am particularly fond of the free-standing timber spiral stair which is a feature of the entrance hall - a beautiful piece of joinery. To the rear are the remnants of some cottages which probably predate the house, and which could suggest that even Bridge House was the remodelling of an earlier house or houses.

Another house of about 1720 is Welshmill Lodge - another "country house" of the time. This was severely remodelled around 1800, and little earlier detail remains: the fine fireplace there, which was specifically mentioned in the statutory listing of the property, actually came from Monmouth House (according to Ronald Vallis, the architect who lived in the Lodge for much of the 20th Century, but who had an office in Monmouth House for a while). By contrast, the first local Poor House was nearby, recorded by 1727! Further out of the town were Nos 2 and 4 Rodden Road, which may either have been a small weaving establishment or a rope works, and Nos 21 and 22 Fromefield, signifying the start of another little hamlet just outside the town.

Just at the end of the period under consideration comes one of Frome's finest houses: the Vicarage to St John's Church, built by the Revd Lionel Seaman in 1744-49. Seaman was not only the town vicar, but also Lord of the Manor of Frome as well, and it seems that he wished to live up to his station! He demolished the old vicarage, but we do not know whether it was on the present site, or on the other side of the road, where the glebe lands are, and where the old Tithe Barn and Bailiff's House stood[4].(A house in King Street, later used by the Ellenbray Press, was called Old Vicarage House in 1915). As we have already seen, Seaman wanted to overhaul the church fabric, but may have been embarrassed by Nathaniel Ireson's scheme to pull down the church and build a new one, a scheme which was rejected by the parish. I feel that, as a "consolation prize", Seaman got Ireson to design him a new vicarage instead: certainly the building has many of Ireson's "trade marks", such as the multiple keystones and Gibbsian surrounds to the main windows. However, if the Revd Skinner's 1821 sketch of the building is to be believed (and he was not beyond a little artistic licence) the vicarage was much smaller than the present-day building: there was obviously a remodelling of the centre portion in Regency times, but the Revd Bennett extended the house on both sides, also adding a chapel to the rear, as well as the porch, a scaled down triumphal arch which is really too heavy for the building. Sadly, at the time of writing, the Vicarage has been sold, and the vicar now lives in a newer house much further away from the church, breaking an historical tradition of perhaps 1300 years!

And so, as we have seen, Frome continued to grow and reflect its prosperity in the first half of the 18th Century, even if much of the building was still on a relatively humble scale. During the second half of the century there was a slowing-down of development, but there were still some interesting new houses being built, which will be featured in the next chapter.

FOOTNOTES

The Statutory List for Frome is the major source of information for this chapter, but particular sources used are as follows:

1. Derek Gill: "The Sheppards and Eighteenth Century Frome": Frome Society for Local Study, 1982
2. Derek Gill: Op. cit.
3. Michael McGarvie: "The Book of Frome: Barracuda Books, 1980
4. Michael McGarvie: Op. cit.

## UPPER BATH STREET, WITH THE FORMER ROOK LANE CHAPEL

The chapel, of 1707, and the houses, up to a century older, originally fronted directly onto Rook Lane: they gained gardens when the new "South approach" to the town (Bath Street) was cut through in 1810-1816. (David Partner)

## WESTBROOK HOUSE, No 33 VICARAGE STREET

A house of c 1700, it originally faced onto a different street, and its "front" is now behind Blindhouse Lane. (A R Yeates).

## Nos 14 TO 16 WILLOW VALE

A row of three fine houses c 1720 - some of the first houses in Frome proper to be built "across the river".

## FROMEFIELD HOUSE

Built by George Sheppard when he married in 1797, and part of the grandest estate which ever existed in Frome.

## COLLEGE PLACE, WALLBRIDGE

John Sinkins' fine house of c 1790, which later became a school, and is now sudivided into several houses.

## THOMAS BUNN'S GRAVE IN CHRIST CHURCH CHURCHYARD

Last resting place of Frome's greatest visionary (architecturally speaking!), who lived from 1767 to 1853. (Terry Cliss)

### SHEPPARD'S BARTON

A group of 18th and 19th Century houses built by the Sheppard family for some of their workers.

### FORMER ST. JOHN'S VICARAGE, VICARAGE STREET

The Revd. Lionel Seaman's house of 1744-49, quite probably designed by Nathaniel Ireson of Wincanton, but twice remodelled in the 19th Century. (G F J Russell)

# CHAPTER THIRTEEN
# THE LATER EIGHTEENTH CENTURY HOUSES OF FROME

After the hectic growth of Frome between 1650 and 1750, the rate slows down considerably, and there are few completely new roads appearing on both the 1774 and the 1813 maps of the town. There was more infilling development, and some remodelling or rebuilding: it was only right at the end of the period under consideration that North Parade was formed to bypass Bridge Street, as the first stage of the reshaping of the street plan of central Frome. There was a little more building along the Portway, Keyford and Broadway; Welshmill and Fromefield also see a few more houses.

Even in this period we are not able to date many houses very firmly, but we have to rely on the style of each house, which normally gives us a limit of 10-15 years either way of a central date. A typical example of stylistic dating is No 13 Bridge Street, which is no later than about 1750. This has a splendid Georgian façade, but the side and rear are less elaborate, suggesting that at one time there was another house alongside (and the numbering would also suggest this). This house was, at least in the 19th Century, the house of the Market Bailiff, who collected tolls on cattle and goods brought into the town (just as the landlord of the Kings Head Inn did on goods coming in from the opposite direction): opposite the house there is still a cast iron plaque which defines the boundary of the town parish and the start of the turnpike trust road (formed in 1757)[1].

A house of a substantial 1754 reshaping (although it also has a 1693 datestone) is No 10 Whittox Lane, marking one of the links between the old and new towns. This was originally owned by the Wickham family, and later by the Browns, the builder family. This house was surprisingly little altered inside, with some good panelling and shell-hood cupboards until a recent fire, although the rear portion has been modified. Other houses of about this date are in Sun Street and Catherine Hill. In or about 1755 Nos 5 to 7 South Parade were built (No 7 having been formerly two houses). Samuel Humphries, who ran a carding factory on the other side of the road, lived at No 6 from 1800, and he modified the roofs of Nos 4 to 7, possibly to match the manse at No 12, which was built (or rebuilt) in 1790. South Parade was a fashionable address for many years, and a number of local worthies lived there. No 7 has a particularly colourful history, being a private school for some years until the late 1880s, when it became a home for the town's trained nurses (the hospital at that time being in Castle Street), and has belonged to the Frome and District Club and Institute since 1909 (their new club premises were erected in the garden of No 7 in 1983).

Another substantial house which has also had a colourful history is No 12 Gentle Street, Argyll House (the whole story has been thoroughly recorded by Michael McGarvie, and I will only summarise some of his information)[2]. The house was built in 1766-67 for Mary Jesser (whose family, first recorded in Frome in 1602, ran a mill and dyehouse at Welshmill). It was in the height of fashion, and would not have been out of place in Bath, even though the idiom of the Venetian window is perhaps overused. It is likely that the rubble stonework of the façade was once rendered, but this has been removed. Internally it has some fine joinery, particularly the staircase, which is in the chinoiserie style. One of its owners, Thomas Lacey, a builder who died about 1830, (and who built both Oriel Lodge next door and Argyll Chambers below), adapted the roof to a mansard to give more accommodation at second floor level. The house name comes from the Dowager Duchess of Argyll, a great admirer of the Revd Bennett, who lived there from 1855 to about 1860 (by which time her Tractarian leaning had prompted her to join the Roman Catholic Church): the name of the house first appears in 1874, the year of her death. As I have already mentioned, it served in place of the George Hotel for a time while the latter was being substantially remodelled: from 1923 to 1933 it was the local tax office. It was very carefully restored by Mr and Mrs N Maggs, who lived there from 1933, and both died there, Mrs Maggs surviving until 1997.

Just up Gentle Street and around the corner is Fairlawn House, No 9 Christchurch Street East. This too is a house with a varied history: its origins are uncertain, but it could be as early as the 17th Century. However, it received at least a substantial remodelling around 1770. At one time it was the Bell Inn, but it ceased as an inn in 1832: it may be that it was the relocated inn from the forecourt of St John's Church of the same name. It later became the court office, and then had varied uses in the 20th Century, during which its condition deteriorated and it had several waves of repair. The rear of the house is older, but the front is essentially later 18th Century work, and it may well have had another remodelling after 1832. The two portions have considerably different ceiling heights at both levels: the rear is low, the front lofty, and this has led to a chaotic arrangement at first floor level, where each of the principal bedrooms has to have a separate stair off a central landing. The main staircase is of 1770, as is at least one of the fireplaces; another fireplace to the rear was of distinctly earlier date, and this has been relocated in one of the principal rooms. An unusual feature is the oak front door: it is one of a series of c1770 in Frome, with shaped upper glazed lights and cross-bracing in the lower panel: other examples are Argyll House, and Garston House and until the 1980s Catherine Hill House had a similar door.

Two town centre houses of this period are Monmouth House and Ken House, in Cork Street. Monmouth House is next door to that in which the Duke of Monmouth stayed in 1685: it is possible that it was finished and named to commemorate the centenary of that event, although I think it is a little earlier than 1785. Cuzner refers to a local tradition of there being a priory in the Cork Street Area, and specifically states"… of which there now remains but a small portion, which is converted into a cellar within the house formerly occupied by the late Thomas Bunn, Esq. A subterranean passage connected this building with a nunnery dedicated to St Catherine, on Catherine Hill, the chapel of which, formerly of considerable capacity, is now transferred into several tenements[3]." Was it usual for a priory and a nunnery to be thus linked? There is no other supporting evidence, and I am afraid that Cuzner was letting his imagination run away with him! As for the tunnel itself, is this the same tunnel that has also appeared under Catherine Hill House, and/ or does it link to No 7 Trinity Street? Monmouth House was, of course the home of the celebrated Thomas Bunn (1767-1853), who so influenced Frome affairs in the late 18th and early

19th Centuries, and was probably built by his father. Alas, most of the interior was stripped out in the mid 20th Century, but a curiosity remaining in the hall is a series of plaster casts, replicas of parts of the Parthenon in Athens made by Henning and dated 1819, set as a frieze. Ken House, next door, likewise had no direct connection with the late Bishop Ken, who died in 1711, whereas the house is at least 50 years after that date. This house too has been gutted internally, although the exterior has been little changed.

About 1780 what might be seen as another version of Argyll House was erected by Mr Houston, a surgeon; this is West Lodge, on the corner of Christchurch Street West and Weymouth Road. This house has the distinction of being the home of successive members of the medical profession for almost 250 years, although the present owner, Dr J E U Moxon, will be the last to have practised from there[4]. The house again features Venetian windows, although somewhat scaled down, as they were apparently going out of fashion; the windows were glazed with "Y" pattern glazing bars instead of the radial glazing at Gentle Street. At some time the sidelights of the ground floor windows have been raised level with the centre light, which looks somewhat odd. The central doorway has a fine swan-neck pediment with an urn, in a rather more sophisticated version of the two similar pediments to the Pack Horse Inn opposite! The large bow window is a 20th Century insertion into the side of what was the original surgery and office (which had side steps down into Christchurch Street - traces of these may still be seen in the street wall). In the early 20th Century this room was absorbed into the house, a new flat-roofed surgery being built on the other side of the house, with an entrance in Weymouth Road: this remained in use until the Frome Health Centre was opened in 1969, and was later converted into a service flat, before being adapted in 2003 as part of a new house. The interior of the house retains its panelling, stairs and other original features. Another house with variations of the Venetian window style may be seen just outside Frome on the Warminster Road; however this is a less sophisticated version.

One of the bigger houses in Frome, North Hill House, was erected in 1763 by Timothy Lacey, a mercer who had married one of the Sheppard daughters in that year[5]. The architect for the house was a relation, William Jesser (1734-1774). However, this house was modified in the early 19th Century by the rebuilding of the roof to form an attic storey. The house has been much altered: in 1955 it was acquired from the Le Gros family by the Frome Urban District Council for use as their offices, and subsequently was used by Mendip District Council until all their offices were transferred to Shepton Mallet. The premises remained as offices until a recent major refurbishment, when it became a private school. It is interesting to note that this house was mirrored, in name, by South Hill House (on the site of what is now the Memorial Theatre) and by West Hill House, in Cork Street (which for some years served as the St Louis Convent), as well as East Hill (just above Wallbridge, now a nursing home): all of these houses appear at about the same time, in the second half of the 18th Century.

About 1790 the Adam style arrived in Frome (although one ceiling in the slightly earlier North Hill House was distinctly of this fashion), and several houses are in this idiom. The first of these, and in some ways the finest, is Welshmill House, Welshmill Road, which was built by Robert Mears, a dyer: it later became the home of James Clement, a clothier, and then of Henry Miller, the entrepreneur who built Dungarvan Buildings in the Market Place. Sadly, the house has long been divided into two, with the best rooms in the western half. Here the corner room has a fireplace and appropriate plasterwork of the period, and there is a fine staircase. Very similar to this house is College Place, Wallbridge (now Nos 7-11 Wallbridge), which served as the home of John Sinkins the clothier, before becoming a school for a while. This house, too, has sadly been divided up. The group is echoed, in a rather humbler fashion, by Trinity Parade (Nos 5, 6, 7 and 11 Goulds Ground), which also must have a date of around 1790.

However, the most impressive of the late 18th Century houses in Frome was Fromefield House, built by George Sheppard in 1797 in very extensive grounds on the edge of town. It was unusually well endowed for Frome: it had its own spring for a water supply, and had a separate bath house (demolished in 1960 to make way for the development of Spring Road and Leys Lane), and also an ice house[6]. The grounds were maintained by no less than 11 gardeners, and the Sheppards had so many staff that in 1834 Mrs Shepppard built a little school opposite (Nos 2 and 4 Bath Road) to educate her servants' children. The house itself has an Adamesque exterior, and could well have been designed by the same person responsible for Welshmill House and College Place; the interior, which must have been equally splendid, is now difficult to appreciate, as the house was divided into ten flats in the mid-20th Century.

Architecturally, we now arrive at what is known as "the battle of the styles"; and whilst, thanks to Thomas Bunn (of whom more in a minute), classicism still dominated new building in Frome for the next 60 years or so, we find the first Gothic revival building (influenced by Walpole's Strawberry Hill, in London) appearing in Frome just around 1800. Whilst the last of our datable Georgian Houses, Garston House (now the veterinary surgery), which was erected in 1796/97, is still completely classical in style, its neighbour, Garston Lodge, built sometime before 1813 (indeed part of its structure could be mediaeval), is decidedly "Gothick". Garston House was built by John Douglas Middleton, a banker who also operated a carrier service between Frome and London[7]. It had an appropriately dignified façade, featuring another of the oak front doors in the style which appeared at Argyll House; inside it has a grand staircase, and one fine room with enriched cornice and columnar decoration. On the other hand, Garston Lodge was allowed to deteriorate very badly during the second half of the 20th Century (after suffering the indignity of having a shopfront set into the side gable wall early in the century), but has now been renovated. It is in the form of a Gothic castle, with battlemented parapets and side gables, and Tudor-style windows and porch: the margined glazing of the windows rather suggests a late 19th Century overhaul. The only other significantly "Gothick" (or Gothic revival) building in Frome is in Cork Street, which is of later date, and the extension to North Hill Cottage. Another important house of this period was Keyford Elms, close to Keyford crossroads. It is recorded in the later 18th Century, but was substantially remodelled in the 1840s, when it became the Christ Church Vicarage, and again in the 1880s. (It remained the vicarage until 1934, when the bachelor Prebendary Edwards became vicar and found it to be too large, and the vicarage was removed to the house on the corner of Christchurch Street West and Park Road, where it remained until the 1970s: a subsequent vicar found it too small, and a house in Somerset Road was purchased instead. Once again, this house proved too big for the current Diocesan standards, and it was sold off during a long interregnum during which period Christ Church had been merged with St John's: the diocese was subsequently forced to buy No 73 Weymouth Road as the current vicarage when the former parish status was restored).

I must not fail to mention some of the smaller houses which almost certainly belong to the period in question.. These include a group of houses in Christchurch Street East, particularly Nos 52 to 56 (the last of these having a pointed-arched central upper window, which is matched by a similar house on Butts Hill, and suggests a 1790 date for all of these); Sydney House, Christchurch Street West (which has another such central window, as well as two-storied bay windows to each side, which I believe are otherwise without parallel in Frome, although there are several similar in Warminster). A number of the houses in Catherine Hill and Catherine Street, Paul Street and Stony Street are likely to have been built or renovated during this period. There are also some more houses in Fromefield, such as No 2, Abergele, which has a fine Ionic portico, a good staircase and an integral coach house. No 30, Garden House, slightly simpler, but still an attractive house (but with an interesting roof frame which is almost a "raised cruck" construction, which is a hark back to a style more common at least 200 years previously, and which could suggest earlier origins). Finally there is a small group of houses in Vicarage Street, including Nos 15, 23, 24 and 25, and the houses on the new North Parade, which was formed in 1797, particularly those on the north-west side, which are all of a piece.

I can not close this chapter, however, without reference to what "might have been" in Frome. I have already made reference several times to the influence exerted by Thomas Bunn in the reshaping of the town centre; of his vision of the opening-up and the rebuilding of the Market Place as a Greek "agora", and of the formation of North Parade (1797), Bath Street (1814-20) and the rebuilding of The Bridge (1821). But this was not all. Bunn loved Bath, and he did not see why his native Frome should not be just as attractive. He envisaged another through road, starting with that part of Sheppards Lane which he had renamed South Parade, cutting through to the Market Place via Stony Street but the levels would have been very unfavourable for such a road, and it came to nothing. However, this did not stop Bunn (a wealthy lawyer who did not, in fact, practise) from planning a rival to Bath's Royal Crescent, (which had been finished in 1775)[8] to give Frome some first-class houses. He acquired land on the south side of Behind Town (Christchurch Street West), including part of the Golden Knoll, on which he was going to build his own crescent. One end would link up with the old Rook Lane, at what is now the entrance to Wesley Slope (presumably this was before Bath Street was envisaged), and the other with the grand avenue which South Parade was to become. He marked out his crescent, and built two pairs of elaborate gate piers at the entrances to the crescent. At this point one of the major backers for the scheme died, and the others pulled out, and the scheme was never built[9]. The South Parade piers survived until the Public Offices were built in 1891; one of the Wesley Slope piers still survives in position, as a poignant reminder of what might have been one of Frome's crowning glories. One of the other piers, found in pieces in a nearby garden, has recently been restored to its proper position at the other end of the proposed crescent, close to the boundary between the public offices and Christ Church churchyard, so that the scope of this ambitious idea can once again be appreciated.

FOOTNOTES

1. Peter Belham: "The Making of Frome": Frome Society for Local Study, 1973

2. Michael McGarvie: "Argyll House, Frome: A Family and Architectural history: Frome Society for Local Study, 1979

3. Samuel Cuzner: "Handbook to Froome Selwood": Cuzner, 1866

4. Michael McGarvie: "The Book of Frome": Barracuda Books, 1980

5. Michael McGarvie: Op. cit.

6. Peter Belham: Op. cit.

7. Michael McGarvie: Op. cit.

8. Walter Ison: "The Georgian Buildings of Bath", 1946, reprinted by the Kingsmead Press in 1969

9. Peter Belham: Op. cit.

## ARGYLL HOUSE, GENTLE STREET
Mary Jesser's fine house of 1766-67.

## No 13 BRIDGE STREET
Of about 1750, this was the home of the Market Bailiff who collected the tolls on goods brought into Frome.

**MENDIP/WELSHMILL HOUSE**
One of several Adam-style houses in Frome of c 1790, now subdivided.

**BRUNSWICK PLACE, FROMEFIELD**
Nos 31 to 33: the poetess Christina Rossetti ran a dame school in No 32 for a while in the 1850s.

# CHAPTER FOURTEEN

# EARLIER NINETEENTH CENTURY FROME HOUSES

It is hardly surprising that, when Frome's economic history is taken into account, there were more houses built in the town, both large and small, in the first third of the 19th Century than in the remainder of that period. When the depression in the woollen industry really began to bite, after the conclusion of the Napoleonic Wars, there was no money to invest in new buildings, and it was really quite late in that century before things really picked up again. There are three useful maps which show the development of Frome over the period: the 1774 map, the earliest known map of the town in a sketchy and diagrammatic form; the measured survey by Mr Cruse of most of the town, dated 1813; and the map showing the revised parish boundary of 1831; these show the growth of the town in this period very well.

By 1831 Broadway had been developed along most of its length, and there were a few houses at the bottom of Nunney Road (some of which were cleared to make way for Frome's first council houses after the First World War). More houses had appeared along Vallis Way, with roads off, such as Horton Street and Button Street, as well as Wiltshire's Barton (roughly where Dorset Close is now): most of the houses on the side roads were very small. Some more houses appeared along The Butts, and again there were small houses in new side roads, such as Water Lane and Somerset Lane (as it was then): again many of these were small, and a number have now been demolished. There were also isolated terraces of houses in the area, including some at The Grove, Albion Place (in what used to be called Puddingbag Lane), and at Hellicars Grave (Whitewell Road). Further out, along the Shepton Mallet Road in an isolated spot, the "Plaguey House" was built on the corner of Sandys Hill Lane (near Messrs Sainsbury's store). This was later relocated to what is now the site of the flats at the end of Delmore Road, and on this same site some unexplained foundations, possibly of the Tudor period, were found when those flats were built around 1970.

Further building occurred along Keyford, and again there were small side roads such as Crown Gardens and Redland Terrace (this last being datable to 1816/1817). Phoenix Terrace, at the top of Catherine Street (Nos 1-18) used to bear a painted date which, if I remember rightly, was 1813 or 1816. The group known as "Newington Butts" in The Butts is rather similar, but a little earlier. There is also the small group of houses forming a complete hamlet at Innox Hill, between Frome and Spring Gardens, of which more later. There was the occasional larger house as well, such as Phoenix Hall (now part of a sheltered housing complex off Dommetts Lane). However, this quarter of Frome was the main area of growth; there were few new houses to the north, east and south of the town, and where they do occur they are mostly larger houses with big grounds.

The Sheppard family, who were by far the biggest employers in the town, built a number of small houses in the town, not exclusively for their own workers, as would appear from the occupations quoted in rate books. What is now known as Sheppard's Barton had already been started in the 18th Century, but there was possibly a weaving shed on the site of Nos

2-6 until about 1820, when the whole barton was reshaped, although Nos 1, and 9-11, were apparently not completed until 1840-1841[1]. However, to accommodate key workers from the Spring Gardens Mill, they also built the 26 houses at Innox Hill. The mill itself had been built in 1809 and extended in 1815 and 1824, and must have been responsible for the larger part of their output. However, the workforce had to come from Frome (as many established footpaths from the Trinity Area to Spring Gardens still testify), and this latter development would have ensured that some hands were close by the mill. It is probable that these houses were built between 1810 and 1830. Although rather humble cottages, they are attractively laid out in an open quadrangle on the side of the hill, of which the changing levels are well exploited, and, of course, they were really out in the countryside when they were built. They are a very interesting fore-runner of such industrial housing as Port Sunlight and other later 19th Century "garden city" developments: sadly the cottages, virtually unaltered when I first knew them in the 1960s, were much exploited when Improvement Grants were made available for their updating: had there been a comprehensive plan for this group drawn up at the time this might well have been another outstanding conservation area, at least as important as the Trinity Area - but it is all too easy to criticise from hindsight!

We must remember, however, that the town centre was also being greatly reshaped during this period, and that Bath Street was built between 1811 and 1816, with houses and shops combined, for the most part: as we have already seen, these are in a classical form, probably architect-designed. The form of these new buildings was obviously seen as being "fashionable", and a number of premises in Stony Street, Catherine Hill, King Street and even Cheap Street had new façades planted on to match. The Town Bridge was shortly to follow, in 1821, all in the same style; and it is interesting to speculate how much influence Thomas Bunn had on the redevelopment of the town during this period, knowing his great love of all things Greek.

Nos 3 and 4 Fromefield also fit into the pre-1813 slot, as does Innox Hill House, where again a rather austere classical style prevails. Another group of fairly substantial houses is Nos 17-20 Portway, which are in the same style. However, Nos 31-33 Fromefield are more reminiscent of Bath or Cheltenham, with their Regency ironwork balconies to the first floor, and these retain some good internal details, including staircases - that to No 31 is still housed in a turret to the rear. No 32 also has a small claim to fame in that the young Christina Rossetti lived there for about 18 months in the 1850s, and for a short while ran a little school there. (In the 1980s the then owner of this house found a number of slate pencils under his floor!)

Turning to the larger houses of the period, Oriel Lodge in Gentle Street just qualifies, having been built in 1800. The façade is still very much in the classical style, and the plan is somewhat conservative, with a separate stair turret to the rear similar to those being built at least 120 years earlier; however the house has been considerably modified internally. A number of the other larger houses are not documented, and so are more difficult to date; however the 1813 map is useful in identifying a number of houses which existed by then. Keyford House, right on the edge of old Frome (near the Keyford crossroads), is one such house: it appears to be an early 19th Century reshaping of an 18th

Century house, with some 1887 additions: the principal elevation is one of the few Gothic revival façades in the town, but the interior has some Regency style rooms. Garston Farmhouse also existed by 1813: this is a rather plain building, albeit still in a classical style, and in some ways is similar to Stoneleigh House at Fromefield (later the regional offices of the Hanson Group), which is also shown on the 1813 map; this latter has been much modified, including a probable realigning of the roof to a lower slope.

A house for which we do have a positive date is Fountain House, built in Cut Hedges Lane (now Gould's Ground) in 1818. This is in the classical style, with a fine garden front (albeit facing north) featuring a segmental bow. It dominates the area, overlooking Holy Trinity Church, which was only erected some 20 years later: not surprisingly it soon became the vicarage for that church, and remained so until 1940. An 1840s school and church room were attached to it on the southern side, in a Tudor Gothic style, but these were demolished about 1970. Most of the internal features remain, despite late 19th Century and 1970s modifications. Not far away is another fine house of pre-1813 date, Conigre House in West End. This was built for Edward Barnard, who at the time owned much of the Trinity Area[2]. It has a Doric entrance portico, and inside there is an elegant staircase and other Regency style trimmings, but it was extended and slightly modified later in the century.

A house in the contrasting Gothic revival style (of which there are not many in Frome) is North Hill (not to be confused with North Hill House next door): this has been considerably modified inside, but it retains a contemporary staircase. Other examples of this style include Garston Lodge, in Christchurch Street East (mentioned in the previous chapter); Selwood Lodge, on Packsaddle, which has a romantic Gothic feel to it, extending to the interior; and Innox Hill Cottage (No 35 Innox Hill), which is very much the cottage orne, and which served as the lodge house to Innox Hill House when built. (These last two houses date from around 1820.)

Going back to the classical style, Knoll House (between Gentle Street and Bath Street) was built in 1839 (on part of the site which James Wickham III had cleared to improve the outlook from his house in Gentle Street nearly 100 years earlier) by a Dr Bush for his son[3]. Not long before he died in 1904, Joseph Singer moved out from West End into this house: his son Edgar bequeathed it to the Royal British Legion in 1945. The Legion altered the house somewhat, in particular with an unsympathetic 1960s extension to one side: sadly the local club could no longer afford to keep it going, and the whole site has been redeveloped. Another similar house is to be found in Spring Road: Spring Grove, which is described as "newly built" in 1840 (and which does not appear on the 1831 map). This was built by the Sheppard family for Miss Susan Sheppard, so that she could live conveniently close to Fromefield House, the family home[4]. This is well detailed, with the kind of well-mannered façade that suggests it was designed by one of the Bath architects.

An area which was fashionable at this time was Vallis Way, and apart from Fountain House, already mentioned, several quite grand houses were erected here, overlooking the river valley. These include Rowden House, which survived as a family house until 1948, when the County Council took it over as a residential nursery; but after major refurbishment and extension in the 1960s it became an old people's home: despite adaptations, much of the central portion retains contemporary detail. Nearby, No 14 Vallis

Way, complete with coach house (now converted into separate dwellings) is another fine example: its style suggests it may be a little earlier, possibly 1820, but it received considerable alteration in the later 19th Century.

Some of the later houses described in this chapter may have been in the fortunate position of being lit by mains gas, thanks to the drive and foresight of the Cockey family, who set up the Frome Gas Company in 1831. This is very early for a small town, and this must have had a certain social cachet. In fact, it came at a most fortunate time, because the depression was soon to come to Frome, and just a few years later there would not have been the money to invest in such a brave new project. Indeed even in 1831 the parish was having to support the emigration of some poor families, and although the railway arrived in 1850, things were very slow to pick up again, as we shall see in the next chapter.

FOOTNOTES

1. Derek Gill: "The Sheppards and Eighteenth Century Frome": Frome Society for Local Study, 1982.

2. Michael McGarvie: "Frome Place Names, their Origins and Meaning", Frome Society for Local Study, 1983 (subsequently revised and enlarged).

3. Michael McGarvie: "The Book of Frome": Barracuda Books, 1980.

4. Michael McGarvie: "Frome Through The Ages": Frome Society for Local Study, 1982.

## MRS SHEPPARD'S FORMER SCHOOL AT FROMEFIELD

Now Nos 2-4 Bath Road, this little school was built to educate the children of the Sheppard family's servants from the big house opposite.

## FROME MARKET PLACE

A nostalgic view taken probably about 1950 - little has changed in the intervening time.

123

CHAPTER FIFTEEN

# LATER NINETEENTH CENTURY HOUSES IN FROME

There are a few problems in dating houses in Frome after 1840, because the cut-off point for the statutory lists of historic buildings (a useful source for dating) is still effectively 1840, although a number of outstanding buildings of later date (albeit very few in Frome) have been scheduled. Until relatively recently, it was unfashionable to research the Victorian and Edwardian periods and beyond, and so references to new houses (as opposed to public buildings, which can usually be picked up from the local press of the time) are few. This means that many have to be dated purely on stylistic grounds. However, for Frome there is one saving grace: the large scale Ordnance Survey maps of 1886[1] will show whether or not a building was standing by that date. These beautifully engraved maps have a wealth of detail: street furniture, garden layouts, etc are all recorded, but sadly the maps were to become out-of-date very quickly.

Nationally, the second half of the 19th Century was a period of enormous building development, and it soon became evident that there was a need to control building to some extent to prevent the erection of more jerry-built housing which had occurred particularly in the big cities. The introduction of standard Building Bylaws in 1875 sought to redress this, and from this date onwards formal plans had to be submitted to the local Board to ensure compliance with the Bylaws. Whilst records of early applications do not always survive, they are a source of information on building dating (although buildings were not necessarily built in the year that the plans were submitted, and sometimes not built at all!). One major impact of the Building Bylaws was to ensure that new buildings incorporated some form of damp proof course (not commonly found before this date), and that where buildings were joined together there was adequate party wall separation (although there are still some party walls in Frome which are no more than stud partitions - and they can not all be the result of sub-division of larger houses!).

Another significant development which was beginning to have some effect was the incorporation of the Royal Institute of British Architects, in 1834. This gradually led to the provision of properly trained architects who were educated not only in design skills but in formal building construction: up to this time architecture had been a hobby of design only for the rich and dilettante, and construction was left to the master mason or master carpenter. Often the skills of either design or construction had been lacking in buildings (some would argue that this can often still be the case!). Gradually trained architects became available locally, although it is doubtful if some of the locally practising "architects" in the 19th Century had any formal training. Joseph Chapman jr of Frome was essentially a master mason rather than an architect, although he is sometimes styled as such: J W Stent, of Warminster, who did some work in Frome in the mid-19th Century, is also unlikely to have been formally-trained, although I have not been able to establish this for sure. By the end of the century, there were two architects practising in Frome, according to the local directories. The first was W George Brown, of St Martins, Park

Road (a house which he designed himself, and thus gives us a clue as to the designer of many late 19th Century houses in the town); he was related to the building firm of F and G Brown, who had restored St John's Church in the 1860s. He died in 1911. The second was J Ace Benyon, who practised from Nunney Road well into the 1930s. However, as we have seen in earlier chapters, architects from outside the town were often used in preference to local architects, a practice which persists to this day - probably 85% of my own work was outside Frome!

There were a number of building firms active in house developments, especially towards the end of the 19th Century. Whereas F and G Brown were the most prominent in the middle of the century, by the end Hodders and Sewards were the principal builders of houses. The quality of the houses built towards the end of the 19th Century and up to the First World War was very high - and with few exceptions was not equalled either before or after this period, certainly not in speculative housing. The firm of F J Seward was founded in 1873; by 1900 they were established in The Butts, and they continued in business until 1966 when the firm was sold: trading continued under two new names for a short while, but these firms soon closed. Sewards were responsible for building houses in The Butts (almost always in pairs), on the West side of the lower section of Weymouth Road (again mostly in pairs, but with some terraces), and Somerset Road, which began with a terrace of relatively small houses from the junction with Whitewell Road, and gradually got bigger as they reached Victoria Park, although most were still built in pairs rather than being completely detached. Their 19th Century houses probably concluded with Nos 32-35, the two largest pairs: the remaining developments in both Weymouth Road and Somerset Road were mostly post-1920. The houses were "modern" in design, most of them allowing for a scullery and some attic accommodation for a servant or two, but externally, although the core was of brickwork, the façades were still of local stone with ashlar dressings, sometimes with a fair degree of carved detail.

Hodders, who were based in Nunney Road, were building similar houses, again mostly in pairs, in Nunney Road, Portland Road and that area of the town, whilst similar houses appear in Bath Road, Locks Hill, Rossiters Road, Christchurch Street (both East and West). All had a degree of individual design about them, although it is difficult to say whether any were actually architect-designed: an exception is the pair of houses in Park Road, in one of which W George Brown, the architect, lived for some years, and which he had designed himself. Nearly all of these houses were at least stone-faced, but in the last few years of the century economics, especially for small houses, were dictating that brick should be used instead of stone for facing, and from this point onwards the face of Frome was changed. One of the earliest brick constructions was Badcox Parade, which consisted of shops with apartments over, although even here there were stone dressings, including some carving. Sewards (and probably Hodders), continued to use stone: indeed Sewards maintained their own quarry at Oldford until the 1930s, and it is likely that most local builders would have had their own quarries, which would have made the use of the local forest marble still viable.

However, the railway, which had arrived discreetly outside the town in 1850, at Wallbridge, was one of the main factors for change: all of a sudden it was possible to bring in large quantities of bricks and roofing tiles, from the Bridgwater area especially, and also roofing slates from Wales, all at very competitive prices. Inevitably these materials were going to be adopted, and it is in the Portway area, which links older Frome with the railway station and the former sidings, where brick construction begins in earnest. The large houses in Portway, such as Coalash Walk, and the streets of smaller houses in Garston Road, Wallbridge Avenue, etc. were in brick, still with a few stone dressings, (of a type which could be found anywhere in the country, completely lacking what might be termed the Frome character) although other houses in nearby Alexandra Road, for instance, remained stone-clad. The change seems to have taken place fairly abruptly in the 1890s: prior to this there was probably not much demand for new smaller houses: Frome had a reasonable supply, and thanks to the depression, and then almost total collapse, of the woollen industry in the town, some of the population had emigrated; the population did not grow at all during the period of 140 years from 1821 to 1961. Furthermore, many of the leases on the small houses of the Trinity Area were expiring for the second time over this period, and most work on small houses was seemingly concentrated on refurbishing the existing houses prior to the granting of new leases, or in some cases demolition and replacement of the most dilapidated houses. Only as alternative industries, such as Cockeys with their cast iron, (and who moved some of their production from Bath Street/ Palmer Street to the Garston Area) and Singers with their brass foundry (not to mention Butler & Tanners printing works), began to prosper, was there sufficient confidence to start building again.

A group of small houses which "bucked the trend" of the 1860s was the development on Golden Knoll carried out by the Wesleyan Methodist Church in 1863, and which was illustrated in the "Builder" magazine of that year. These were designed by the architect W J Willcox (about whom little is known) in a semi-Gothic style, and they sit on the site very well, complimenting the church, and providing a schoolroom as well as housing. They were deemed to be of sufficient interest to merit illustration in this magazine during 1863[2].

As for larger houses, these were still being built in various places, although not in any great number. One of the first houses in this period was No 44 Portway, a most individually styled house built by Joseph Chapman jr for both his home and his masonry yard, which has a mass of ornament wilfully combining Gothic and classical details, surely intended to demonstrate his ability to work in any style rather than to display his capabilities for design - (he styled himself as an architect as well as monumental mason, and designed many important buildings in the town): this house dates from 1867. One of the few roads to be developed in the 1870s was the private road serving West End Villas, which is known from 1872[3]. The houses here were middle-class, and again in pairs. Some larger pairs (Rock Hill and Garth Villas - one of the latter now renamed Bromstone) appear in Welshmill Road, and around the same time Orchard Villa was erected in nearby Welshmill Lane; North End House was built at the top of Bridge Street, and Vallis Lodge and Seathwaite Cottage (now Holy Trinity Vicarage) were built in Orchard Street. Further out, Redland Place and Redland Villas appear in The Butts. With the exception of these last examples, most of these houses were on infill sites: the only new road which appears by the time of the 1886 maps was Weymouth Road (formerly Clements Lane), where Waverley and Sydney Villas, as well as Bath Buildings, had been built by this time. (These last were alongside a small quarry, which, although backfilled, has never been built upon).

It could be said that the hallmark of these houses of the late 19th Century was "solid respectability", reflecting the prosperity of the nation (indeed of the British Empire), and the gradual return to a position of good business and full employment in the town, after probably fifty years of depression. However, Frome was still a very compact town, with one of the highest figures of inhabitants per square mile in the country, and although it had been felt necessary to extend the town boundaries in 1831, much of the area within those boundaries was still open fields, and would remain so until the 1950s - in fact it would be 1985 before the boundaries were extended again - but that is part of the 20th Century story, and that is for the next two chapters to tell.

FOOTNOTES
1. OS 1886 map reproduced by Frome Society for Local Study 2011
2. Francis Kelly (investigator for) The Department of the Environment Statutory List of Buildings of Special Architectural Interest: Frome, Somerset, 1983. (This list is used for much of the other detail in this chapter.)
3. Michael McGarvie: "Frome Place Names, Their Origin and Meaning": Frome Society for Local Study, 1983 (subsequently revised and enlarged).

# CHAPTER SIXTEEN
# HOUSES IN FROME FROM 1900 TO 1960

In contrast to many parts of the country, Frome was hardly expanding at all during this period, partly because of the stability of the population figures for the town. In fact, the largest developer was probably the Frome Urban District Council, who, after the First World War found themselves responsible for building houses to rent out to those who could not afford to buy a house of their own. Indeed, in the later 1960s they were to build their 1,000th unit of accommodation (counting bungalows and flats as well as houses), which represented a significant proportion of the town's housing in 1960 - probably about 20-25%.

The private sector had been busy in the early years of the 20th Century, up to 1914, and development continued in the Wallbridge/ Portway/Locks Hill area and in little pockets of land elsewhere. Gradually the pattern of the houses was changing to meet new needs; but the most significant change in Frome was probably the introduction of a mains electricity supply for the town by 1904/05 - relatively early for a small town. Hodders and Sewards were still building, and they had been joined by Barnes: Browns seem to have closed down by about 1900. On the architectural front, W George Brown had died in 1911, although J Ace Benyon continued until the 1930s; but Percy Rigg set up an office in Monmouth Chambers about 1905, and his practice continued until Ronald Vallis bought him out in about 1933; the practice later moved to North Parade. Just after 1918 Lou Webb started practice in the town - initially in partnership with J Coles (the estate agent who also ran the Auction Mart in Vicarage Street) and he continued in the town until the early 1970s. In the early 1950s there was a G Wheeler practising from Nunney Road (possibly continuing Benyon's practice).

After 1918 came the Great Depression, and few new private houses were built until well into the 1930s, but the Frome UDC got going fairly quickly, and soon their housing in Summer Hill (renamed Woodland Road) was to be followed by more in the lower parts of Nunney Road and other small pockets of land. In the private sector, a few larger houses were built in The Butts and Oakfield Road, and some noticeably smaller houses appeared in the extensions of Somerset Road and Weymouth Road, and also along Vallis Road and in Robins Lane; and a few pairs of houses were built in Nunney Road, (with Lynfield Road and the start of Houston Way), Cottles Oak and Egford Hill. One major house built in 1935 to the design of R Vallis, Knoll House in Whitewell Road, has survived almost unaltered since it was constructed, and has recently been "Listed" as being a significant house of the "moderne" style.

However, the most significant development was the exploitation of the northern side of the river for the first time. There had been sporadic development in Welshmill and around Fromefield, but until the 1920s most of the rest was open fields. Some larger houses were constructed along the Bath Road, the top end of Rodden Road, and Berkley Road, and semidetached houses were built in Berkley Road (with the offshoot loop of Windsor Crescent) and in Rodden Road (with Beechwood Avenue; Beechwood Close being added in the 1950s). But the boom in building was short-lived, as by 1939 the country was at war again.

In the aftermath of the Second World War, priority was given to the rebuilding of bomb-damaged areas, and building materials (particularly timber, which was actually rationed for some years) were in short supply: in 1950 there was a two-year delay for Welsh roofing slates, for example. Many substitute materials were used - most proved to be unsatisfactory in the long run. Frome had suffered minimal bomb damage during the war: a house or two at the bottom of Nunney Road being the only casualties, and so Frome's builders were more likely to have been occupied in helping Bath and Bristol to recover from the heavy bombing they endured. The Frome UDC would seem to have had access to more building materials than the private sector, for they soon got going again, and although one or two prefabricated houses were erected in the town, they were soon busy erecting (more or less) traditional housing, (albeit with brick facings rather than the stone which they had used pre-war), except for some houses which relied heavily on precast concrete members. Their houses were erected in several areas including Queen's Road, (off Somerset Road); Cherry Grove and Rossiters Road and Hill; and Singers' Knoll and Randolph Road off Summer Hill. The Council also cleared Wiltshire's Buildings, Chinnocks Buildings and Union Street, the old Badcox Brewery, and parts of Vallis Way and Horton Street to form Dorset Close and the peripheral buildings, and The Leaze was constructed as an offshoot of Robins Lane. But the Council, too, joined in the extension of the town across the river, with a swathe of houses from Rodden Road looping round to Berkley Road, including St John's Road, St Mary's Road, Coronation Road and Boundary Avenue. However, in this last area they were building on the edge of the town, and in extending this estate they actually had to build on land administered by the Rural District Council: Boundary Avenue was exactly that!. In all this probably amounts to some 700 houses - not bad for a small local authority!

By contrast, the private sector was slow to get started. Messrs Hodders and Barnes survived until the 1950s, and Sewards until 1966, but none of them were any longer involved in housing development generally; however, towards the end of the 1950s a new local firm, M Williams and Co (whose yard was at the top of Wesley Slope) became the main developer in the town. There was some development by them in Oakfield Road (including St Aldhelm's Close), and they also built Foster Road and Charles Road off Locks Hill, as well as infill housing elsewhere. Other developments on the south side of the town included some houses in Whitewell Road, and also Stourton View. More houses were built on the north side of the river, and by 1960 Lewis Crescent had been completed and Park Hill Drive started.

Overall, however, things were fairly quiet until about 1960 - but then the whole character of Frome, still a small market town of some 11,200 inhabitants, was to change: the town was to undergo such rapid expansion in the remainder of the 20th Century that by its end the population would have rather more than doubled - a growth the like of which had not been seen since the development of the Trinity Area in 1665-1725, and which would make it look small by comparison - but that is the ground to be covered by my final chapter.

FOOTNOTES

Most of the information in this chapter is gained from the Frome Almanacks and the directories of the period.

# CHAPTER SEVENTEEN
# LATER TWENTIETH CENTURY HOUSES IN FROME

If there had not been official intervention, I doubt whether Frome would have grown so fast in the second half of the 20th Century. Left to the normal laws of supply and demand, the population would probably have increased by two or three thousand, with the need for far fewer houses than were actually built. (Although it must be admitted that much of the town's housing stock at that time was very small and without modern facilities.) On the other hand, if there had not been some form of control, development would have been patchy, and most likely in the form of "ribbon development" which was such a feature of the 1920s and 1930s in many parts of England. A degree of planning control existed before the Second World War (and local architect Ronald Vallis, who also held a degree in Town Planning, was much involved in the planning of Frome before that war), but it was the Town and Country Planning Act of 1947 that really established the planning system that we have today. In theory, the system is a good one, but Frome has suffered in two ways as a direct result: firstly, there has not been sufficient control over the materials used in modern houses, so that whilst a proportion are in stone or "reconstructed stone" and fit in with the local character, all too high a proportion are in bricks of varying colours, so that the edges of Frome look like any other town in England.

The second drawback of the planning system as far as Frome is concerned is the supposed control of housing, employment and infrastructure which is an inevitable result. Two factors persuaded the planners that Frome needed many more houses: one was the need for retirement homes in the South-West, of which, rightly, Frome was to provide its share. The second, which highlights the failure of "Planning", certainly when it is used politically, was the governmental decision made in the early 1970s to relocate the Ministry of Defence to Bath; and because Bath had already reached its natural limits for expansion, the neighbouring towns, including Frome, would have to provide their share of accommodation. By the time a later government changed its mind, and kept the ministry in London, it was too late; many of the houses had already been built, and many more had received planning approval, so the damage had been done. Up to about 1960 there was employment in the town for everyone who wanted to work (although of course some people commuted to Bath or Bristol, and others came into the town to work). By the end of the 1970s, Frome was an unemployment "black spot" (with an unemployment rate of about 12%), and furthermore, although many of the new houses had been built, there had been no alteration to the infrastructure of the town. Two new primary schools had been provided in the 1960s, but the technical college had been first merged with that of Radstock, and then when local government was reorganised, merged instead with Frome Grammar School. A few new shops were provided; a health centre had been built, but the hospital had been downgraded, and so on. To add insult to injury, the seat of local government was removed from Frome in 1974, and the new "unitary authority" of Mendip District Council was set up in the smaller town of Shepton Mallet, on the grounds of being more central to the area governed, rather than in Frome, which is by far the biggest town in the District.

So outside factors decreed Frome's growth, and it duly grew, slowly at first, but the pace of growth accelerated. In the 1960s, the Urban District Council continued to provide housing to rent, but their major work was concerned with the "slum clearance" of the Trinity Area and the rehousing of those moved out from there (more detail is given in Chapter 11) into a new estate on The Mount. The roads concerned were Austin Close, Feltham Drive, Stonewall Terrace, Southfields and Hillside Avenue. This development saw Frome's first (and only) small tower blocks of flats. By the 1970s the council was developing an estate on the opposite side of Frome, in Whatcombe Vale, (Whatcombe Road, Hill Ground & Hodders Close), and it was here that they notched up their 1,000th council house. They had also built a small development in The Grove, off Marston Road, as temporary housing for new "key workers" coming into the town: the successor Mendip District Council subsequently incorporated this into yet another new estate. Another small development of theirs, from about 1970 was Oakfield Close, off Oakfield Road. There was also a perceived need for old persons' accommodation, and they built bungalows in Sunny Side, Green Lane, and Roddenbury Close, as well as flats in Delmore Road, Whitewell Place and at Gorehedge, where a terrace of probably early 19th Century houses was demolished to make way for the flats and a small common room. This was subsequently to be matched in the private sector by the Hanover Gardens development on Critchill.

But the Frome Urban District Council also became involved in a private development. One factor deterring key workers from moving into the town was the lack of "upper middle class" housing in the district, and so they were instrumental in getting the Northcote Estate developed: they provided the roads and the plots: in theory no-one was allowed to buy more than two plots, so that a variety of larger and individual houses would result: in fact one enterprising local development firm bought at least six, and probably more, through nominee purchasers! This area was developed from the early 1960s onwards, using some of the grounds of Northcote House, long since absorbed into what is now Frome College. The original estate comprised Grange Road, Mendip Drive, Selwood Crescent, Northcote Crescent and Mendip Close; it was later extended by the developer firm of Bradleys, who extended Grange Road out to meet Leys Lane, and added Champneys Road, Meadow Road and Tankeys Close.

From 1960 onwards the private sector really got going, but it was beginning to become difficult to find areas of any decent size on which to build houses within the town (bearing in mind that there were still active farms within the town boundary then), and much new building was on relatively small pockets of land. The development of Leys Lane had begun in the 1950s, and it was extended, with more roads being built off from it, including Leystone Close, Park Hill Drive, Clumber Drive, and so on, using land that had once belonged to Fromefield House. The small local builder Sutton built a few houses off Bath Road (on the corner of the Grammar School site), and then had to build outside the town at Styles Hill and Styles Avenue. Mordel Construction (another small local firm, who managed to build several houses on the Northcote Estate) developed Delmore Close, on a pocket of land off Whitewell Road.

131

On the north-east side of Frome, Marston Back Lane, which had just a few farms and houses at the start of the 1960s, was the scene of considerable development, with side roads such as Marston Close and Marston Mead being developed by the local council, and Stourton View, Stourton Close and Stourton Gardens being constructed by private developers.

In the 1970s, some local employers found it necessary to build their own houses for their key workers. Singers built Delta Close, off Welshmill Lane, conveniently close to their factory, and Butler and Tanner built Easthill, off Styles Avenue - an estate of very individual linked bungalows, which were illustrated in the "Architect's Journal" of the day. The Somerset Police Authority also built some houses, in Farrant Road and Goulds Lane, to meet their needs.

The local firm of M Williams and Co. began building on Berkley Down (outside the town then, in the area administered by the Frome Rural District Council) in the early 1960s, with Whitestone and Wynford Roads, crossed by Monmouth Drive and Boundary Road (although the latter soon became Wythburn Road when it entered the estate) which linked into the St John's Road estate of council houses. Other roads followed (as a little conceit on the part of the developers all of the road names here begin with "W" for Williams), and most of the estate was complete by the mid 1970s, when Williams merged with a Guildford firm.

By the 1980s, the larger firms of developers were beginning to take an interest in the town, and they must take some of the blame for the loss of character around the perimeter of the town: they just built their standard house types, which they had used all over England, varying the materials here and there, to make otherwise identical houses look that little bit different. It need not have been so: there were a number of architects in the town by this time: Ronald Vallis stayed in practice until about 1970, but his son W W R (Bill) Vallis had joined him as a partner in 1964, and the firm became firstly Vallis & Vallis, and then Nugent Vallis Brierley, as it expanded and set up a Bath office as well as its North Parade office in Frome. Having been with them for a while, I set up my own practice in 1968, and subsequently (partly due to the tremendous publicity that Frome received in the 1970s when the importance of so many historic buildings in the town, and the threat of demolition which was hanging over so many of them, was being appreciated nationally) a number of architects and surveyors came to the town, some not staying very long. These included Wolstenholmes, the surveyors (Roger Wolstenholme, the founder, retired fairly early, but the firm continues), Bruce Yoell, an architect (also a lecturer at Bath University), Horsfall & Norris (architects), and several one-man firms. Even so, sadly, few Frome buildings of this period were designed by any of these professionals. (Thomas Bunn's observations of 150 years earlier were still horribly appropriate. In his diaries he once noted:

" It is the usual practice of Frome men who have built houses and not employed an architect, calling the builders or carpenters the architect, and with poor results"[1].

Substitute "developers" for "builders or carpenters", and today's position is well summarised!)

Amongst the builders, Sewards survived until 1966, where the head of the firm, F J (Jack) Seward, trained as a building surveyor, and practised as such for some years.

The firm was taken over by WEM Carroll Ltd, and then by Peter Drake of Bath, but by the mid-1970s it had gone. M. Williams continued until around 1990, after merging with another firm, but now Frome has no major firm of general builders, although there are several good small firms still thriving, including Pang Properties, who are developers of problem sites rather than general builders. (Lest there should be any misunderstanding, I must exclude one firm which moved to Frome in 2001, Nimbus Conservation Ltd, a firm of national repute - but they are specialists in historic building work, and not general builders as such!). The Bath firm of M P Kent developed most of Stonebridge before they were taken over by Beazers; Prowtings and Barrett were among the national firms which moved in, and little development after about 1980 was of local character.

I think it is fair to say that there have been no exceptional individual houses built in the town since 1960 (which is not an implication that nothing of quality has been built): indeed the majority of the private houses built since 1960 (apart from the special case of the Northcote Estate, which I have already mentioned) are parts of mostly speculative estates, even though some of the actual houses concerned are larger, with four or even five bedrooms. It will therefore be easier to describe the private development from about 1980 by areas.

The Leys development was followed by the development of the Packsaddle area (on the lands of the former Packsaddle Farm), which adjoined both this and the Northcote Estate, and was begun about 1974. Another large development took place at Innox Hill, and Frome spread almost into Spring Gardens. On the other side of the Bath Road, M P Kent started the Stonebridge Estate on the grounds of what had been Beaconsfield Farm about 1976, the first phase of which gained a government housing award for the layout and general design; apart from Stonebridge Drive and Beaconsfield Way, all the roads were named after trees. Opposite the Berkley Down development, Prowtings developed several roads including Brunel Way (all of their roads were named after railway engineers), and gradually the two estates were joined (and Brunel Way became a through road, much to the dismay of many of the residents, although it had always been planned as such!). Forest Road branched off from Stonebridge Drive, with streets named after birds (except a little close wittily called The Copse). Between Prowtings and the Kent development other builders built a series of roads named after Somerset villages, and the area was virtually completed when Barratts developed Wellow Drive and its offshoots.

Geographical and other restraints meant that there could be little development to the south-east of the town (the railway, and later the town bypass, provided a natural barrier), and likewise there was little scope to the south and west, (where George's Farm closed down to make way for the Marston Trading Estate as well as the small council development of The Grove, Cabell Road, Pinmore Road and the small culs de sac off these) but to the north-west, on Critchill, building continued right to the edge of the escarpment overlooking Nunney, and swallowed up Marston Farm (Courts Barton and the associated roads). Writing in the first edition of this book in 1985, I commented that, with the planning approvals already existing, there was really little land left in the town for further housing unless the areas of special landscape value were to be invaded; and mercifully, so far as reasonable limits imposed by the new town boundaries of 1985 have not been breached.

This meant that the only way to achieve more housing in the town was to develop on "brownfield sites" (sites already occupied by disused buildings, usually industrial) rather than "green" land. In fact, the first "brownfield site" to be developed was that of the old Cronite factory in Marston Back Lane, where Georgian Court was built in the 1970s, but it was to be some while before any major sites were taken over. Small pockets of land, such as the old County Surveyor's yard in Nunney Road and Bennett's Nurseries, in Nunney Road/ Dommetts Lane, were taken over for housing, and of course the Mendip District Council weaved a number of new houses into the Trinity Area redevelopment of the early 1980s, as well as on a small site next door to St John's School in Christchurch Street East. By the 1990s the issue was becoming more significant, and the areas redeveloped gradually became bigger. Mendip District Council cleared and redeveloped the area known as "The Piggeries" between Castle Street and Catherine Street (gaining another housing award in the process). Back with the private sector, Knight's builder's yard at Gorehedge made way for Knights Court, to be followed later by the development of Sewards' old yard in The Butts for Newington Close. Other "brownfield developments" include The Cooperage, on the old Wilson and Scotchman site, the Rook Lane housing on the sites of the former swimming pool and electricity works, and on the site of the former abattoir in Whittox Lane. At the time of writing two larger redevelopments are taking place: on the former Singer's site at West End, (Waterloo), and on the site of the old Wallbridge woollen mill. Planning applications had also been approved for redevelopment on the Slipps Nursery (between Park Road and Butts Hill) and the old Rawlings Factory sites (in Christchurch Street West). However, it becomes more and more difficult to see where any further large-scale housing developments are to take place without breaching the notional boundaries of the town - and to do this would mean the provision of some very costly additional services, because of the general topography around the town - and it may well have to be accepted that Frome can only support a population of around 30,000, (especially with its existing infrastructure) and that further expansion is not feasible: time only will tell!

FOOTNOTES

1. Michael McGarvie: "Frome Through The Ages": Frome Society for Local Study, 1982

The author moved into Frome in 1963, and most of this chapter is based upon his experiences and memory - so he is to be blamed for any inaccuracies!

# BIBLIOGRAPHY

The following is a list of the books and articles consulted during the preparation of this book, each of which would yield further information on the subject of Frome's buildings.

AMERY , Colin, and
CRUIKSHANK, Dan    "The Rape of Britain" (Paul Elek, 1975)

ANON    Frome Directories for 1933, 1949 and 1970-71

ANON    "A History of Frome Cheese Show 1877-1977 (Frome and District Agricultural Society, 1977)

AYRES, James    "Building the Georgian City": (Yale University Press, 1998)

BALCH, Harry:    Article on "Local Government in Frome, Past, Present and Future" which appeared in

"Eighty Years of Frome, 1894-1974" (Frome UDC 1974)

BELHAM, Peter    Article on "A History of the Blue House" appearing in "The Blue House Restored"

(Blue House Appeal Committee" 1965)

BELHAM, Peter    "The Making of Frome" (Frome Society for Local Study 1973)

BELHAM, Peter    "St Aldhelm and the Founding of Frome" (Frome 1300 Publications 1985)

BENNETT, Revd WJE    "History of the Old Church of St John of Froome" (Penny 1866)

CLIFTON-TAYLOR, A    "The Pattern of English Building" (Faber 1972)

CUZNER, Samuel    "Cuzner's Handbook to Froome Selwood" (Cuzner 1866)

DEPARTMENT OF
THE ENVIRONMENT    List of Buildings of Special Architectural or Historic Interest: Frome, Somerset (Compiler: Francis Kelly: Department of the Environment, 1983). The entries in this List are summarised in the Appendix.

DUNNING, Robert    "The Monmouth Rebellion: A Guide to the Rebellion and Bloody Assizes" (Dovecote Press 1984)

FROME SOCIETY
FOR LOCAL STUDY    The Year Books published by this society began in 1987, and have been published at intervals since then, Volume 15 appearing in 2012. They contain many articles and photographs relevant to the material in this book.

GILL, Derek    "The Story of Christ Church, Frome" (British Publishing Co Ltd 1974 - a revised edition now published by the Christ Church PCC)

| | |
|---|---|
| GILL, Derek | "Bath Street, Frome" (Privately published, 1992) |
| GILL, Derek | "Experiences of a 19th Century Gentleman" (Frome Society for Local Study, 2003) |
| GILL, Derek | "Frome School Days" (Frome 1300 Publications, 1985) |
| GILL, Derek | "The Sheppards and Eighteenth Century Frome" (Frome Society for Local Study 1982) reissued on CD 2012 |
| GILL, Derek & BUCKLEY, John | "Willow Vale Frome"(Frome Society for Local Study 2010) |
| GOODALL, Rodney | Article on "The Changing Face of Frome" in "Eighty Years of Frome 1894-1974" (Frome UDC 1974) |
| GOODALL, Rodney | "The Industries of Frome"(Frome Society for Local Study 2009) |
| HARVEY & others | "Harvey's Frome Almanack & Directory" (which commenced in 1846 and continued as "The Frome Almanack & Directory" into the 1930s): a few random years were consulted, viz: 1858, 1865, 1876, 1905, 1915 and 1923 |
| HODDER, Arthur | Article on "Frome in the 1880s" in "Eighty Years of Frome 1894-1974" (Frome UDC 1974) |
| HUDSON, Kenneth | "The Fashionable Stone" (Adams and Dart, Bath, 1971) |
| ISON, Walter | "The Georgian Buildings of Bath" (Kingsmead Reprints 1948/1969) |
| LEACH, Roger & others | "Early Industrial Housing: The Trinity Area of Frome" (Royal Commission on Historical Monuments Supplementary Series Number 3: HMSO 1981) |
| McGARVIE, Michael | "The Book of Frome" (Barracuda Books 1980) |
| McGARVIE, Michael | "Argyll House, Frome: A Family and Architectural History" (Frome Society for Local Study 1979) |
| McGARVIE, Michael | "Frome in Old Picture Postcards" (3 volumes) (European Library, 1983, 1984 & 1985) |
| McGARVIE, Michael | "Frome Past and Present", a volume of archive and up-to-date matching photographs of the town (Rotary Club of Frome Selwood, 1999) |
| McGARVIE, Michael | "Frome Place Names, Their Origin & Meaning" (Frome Society for Local Study 1983, subsequently revised and reprinted) |
| McGARVIE, Michael | "Frome Through The Ages: An anthology in prose and verse" (Frome Society for Local Study 1982) |

McGARVIE, Michael  "Light in Selwood; A Short History of St John's Church, Frome" (Frome Society for Local Study 1976)

ORDNANCE SURVEY  The large scale (1:500) maps of Frome, surveyed 1883 to 1886 republished by Frome Society for Local Study 2011

OVEREND, Eunice  Article on "Frome's Buildings" in "The Blue House Restored" (Blue House Appeal Committee 1965)

OVEREND, Eunice  "The Geology of the Frome Area" (Frome 1300 Publications 1985)

PARTRIDGE, Ann  Article on "Frome Selwood - A Town Founded from Stone, Cloth and Ink" (Somerset & Wessex Life Magazine, June 1973)

PONTING, Ken  "Wool & Water" (Moonraker Press 1975)

R.I.B.A.  Article in the 150th Anniversary Journal of the Royal Institute of British Architects, 1984

RUSSELL, GFJ  "Frome: Then and Now" Frome 1300 Publications 1985

SWEETMAN, George  "History of Wincanton" (Sweetman 1903 or 1904)

TUCKWELL, Rowland  "The Story of the Parish Church, Frome, Somerset" (British Publishing Co Ltd 1946)

VARIOUS  "Frome, a Special Town", a collection of articles about Frome (Rotary Club of Frome 1995)

WHITE, -  "A Short History of Frome" (unknown publisher 1892)

APPENDIX

# A LIST OF THE BUILDINGS OF SPECIAL ARCHITECTURAL OR HISTORIC INTEREST IN FROME PROPER, as compiled by the then Department of the Environment, and confirmed by them in 1983

This list includes subsequent amendments or additions up to December 2012. Most of the buildings listed here are of the standard Grade II; buildings allocated Grade II* are printed in *italics*, and the Grade I buildings are printed in **bold letters**. Some additional items such as gateposts and railings, milestones, the 20 or so Cockey lamp-posts, etc. are not included; neither are items outside the declared town boundary.

| | |
|---|---|
| BADCOX | Nos 6 and 6a |
| BATH ROAD | Fromefield House, Nos 1, 1a, 2, 4, and 6 |
| BATH STREET | Nos 1, 1a, 2, 2a, 3, 4, 5, 6, 7, 8, The Church Screen, *Saint John's Church*, The Bennett Cross, Bishop Ken's Tomb, No 8a, **Rook Lane Chapel**, Nos 10, 11, 12, 13, 14,15, 16, 17, 19, 20, 21,22, 23, and 24 |
| BLIND HOUSE LANE | The Former Lock-up |
| THE BRIDGE | The Town Bridge, Nos 3, 4, 5, 6, 7, 8, and 9 |
| BRIDGE STREET | Nos 1 2; *No 13* Boundary Post opp No 13 |
| BROADWAY | The Royal Oak P.H. |
| BUTTON STREET | Nos 2, 3, 4, 5. 6. 7, 8, and 9 |
| THE BUTTS | Nos 29, 31, 39 and 44 |
| CASTLE STREET | Nos 1,2,3,4,5,6, 7, 9, 20,21,23, The Lamb & Fountain P.H., and No 49 |
| CATHERINE HILL | Nos 1, 2, 3, 4, 5, 6, 8, 9, 12, 13, 14, 15, 16, 17, 18, 19, The Screen to Zion Church, Nos 30, 31, 32, and 33 |
| CATHERINE STREET | Nos 3, 4 (including cottage to rear), 5, The Former Badcox Chapel, The Sun Inn P.H., Nos 10, *11*, 12, 13, 14, 15, 16, 17, 18, 30, 41, 42, and 43 |
| CHEAP STREET | Nos 2 and 3, *No 4*, Nos 5, 6, 7, 7a, 8, *No 11*, Nos 12, 13, 14, 15, 16, 18, 19, 20, 21, 22, 23 and 24 |
| CHRISTCHURCH ST. E. | Fairlawn House, Nos 23, 24, 25, 52, 53, 54, 55, 56, Boundary Mark |
| CHRISTCHURCH ST.W. | The Ship Inn P.H., Nos 11 12, The Pack Horse PH., Nos 20, 21, 25, Sydney House, Rook Lane House, *West Lodge, Christ Church*, The Former Municipal Offices, and The Gate Pier on Wesley Slope |

| | |
|---|---|
| **CHURCH STEPS** | Old Church House |
| **CHURCH STREET** | The Via Crucis to St John's Church, Nos 1, 2, 3, 4, and 7 |
| **CLINKGATE** | Clinkgate Farmhouse |
| **CORK STREET** | Monmouth House, Wool House, No 2, *Nos 3* and *3b*, Ken House, The Old Presbytery, and Conigre House |
| **EAST HILL** | East Hill Cottage |
| **FROMEFIELD** | Stoneleigh House, Nos 2, 3, 4, 21, 22, 30, 31, 32, 33, and 34 |
| **GARSTON LANE** | Garston Farmhouse |
| **GENTLE STREET** | No 1, *The Chantry, The Hermitage,* Nos 3, 4, 7, 8, 9, 10, 11 Oriel Lodge, and *Argyll House* |
| **GOULDS GROUND** | *Fountain House,* Nos 5, 6, 7, 11, 14, 15, 16 and 22 |
| **HIGH STREET** | No 22 |
| **HORTON STREET** | Nos 13, 14, 20, 21, 22, 25, 26, 27 and 28 |
| **INNOX HILL** | Nos 35 and 37, St Mary's Church Hall, Vicarage Gardens |
| **JUSTICE LANE** | The former Drying-house |
| **KEYFORD** | Nos 5, 6, 19, 20, 21, 22, 23, The Crown Inn, *No 25,* Nos 30, 32, 34, 35, 40, 41, 42, 43, 44, The Limes, Nos 46, 52, 54, 55, 56, 57, 58, 59, 60, 61, 62, 63, 64, 62, 66, and 67 |
| **KEYFORD TERRACE** | Nos 1, 2, 3, 4, 5, 6, 7, 8, 9, 10, 11, 12, 13 and 14 |
| **KING STREET** | No 2, The Archangel, *Iron Gates, Court House,* The Three Swans P.H., Nos 16, 17, 18, 23, 24, 25 and 26 |
| **LEYS LANE** | Selwood Lodge |
| **LITTLE KEYFORD LANE** | Nos 8, 9, 11, 11a and Keyford House |
| **LOWER KEYFORD** | No 22, Stonewall Manor, No 35, Keyford Farmhouse, Nos 50, 55, 56, 57, 58, 59, 60, 61, 62, 63, 64, 65, 66 and 67 |
| **LOCKS HILL** | Keyford Elms, No 92 |
| **MARKET PLACE** | Nos 3, 4, NatWest Bank, Coventry B.S., The George Hotel, The Crown Hotel, Nos 7, 8, 9, 10, 11, 12, **The Blue House,** The Blue Boar Inn, Nos 17, 18, 19, 20, 21, Lloyds Bank, No 25 and the Boyle Cross |
| **MERCHANTS BARTON** | The Silk Mill |
| **MILK STREET** | Nos 45, 50 and 50a |
| **THE MOUNT** | Nos 5 and 6 |
| **MOUNT PLEASANT** | Nos 3, 4, 5, 8, 9, 10, 11 and 12 |

| | |
|---|---|
| NAISH'S STREET | Nos 4, 5, 23, 24, 25, 29, 30, 38, 39, 40, 41, 42, 43, 46, 60, 61,62, and 63 |
| NEW BUILDINGS | No 13 |
| NORTH PARADE | The Frome Museum, Nos 2, 2a, 3, 4, 5, 6, 7, 8, 9, North Hill House and North Hill |
| ORCHARD STREET | Nos 5 and 5a |
| PALMER STREET | The Warehouse, Nos 1 and 2 |
| PAUL STREET | Nos 12, 13, 14, 15, 16, 19, 20, 22 and 23 |
| PORTWAY | Garston Lodge, Garston House, Nos 17,18, 19, Montgomery Court, The Railway Station and No 44 |
| RODDEN ROAD | Nos 2 and 4 |
| SCOTT ROAD | Three telephone kiosks |
| SELWOOD ROAD | Nos 17, 18, 24, 25, 29, 30, 31, 72, 73, 74, 75, 77, 78, 79, 80, 81, 82, 83, 84, 85, 86 and 87 |
| SHEPPARD'S BARTON | Nos 1,2,3,4, 5,6, 7, 8, 9, 10, 11, 12, 13, 14, 15, 16, 17, 18, 19, 20,21,22,23 and 24 |
| SOUTH PARADE | Sheppard's Barton Baptist Chapel and schoolrooms, No 1, The Warehouse, Nos 2, 3, 4, 5, 6 and 7 |
| SPRING ROAD | Spring Grove |
| STONY STREET | Nos 1,2,9, 10, 11, 12, 13, 14, 15, *No 16,* and No 17 |
| SUN STREET | Nos 2, 3, 4 (with stable and coach house adjoining), and 13 |
| SUNNYSIDE | Nos 7 and 8 |
| TRINITY STREET | Nos *1, 2, 3,* 11, 15, 16, 17, 18, *Holy Trinity Church,* and the former school |
| TRINITY ROW | No 14 |
| VALLIS ROAD | No 9, Rowden House, No 14 with the coach house, Nos 59, and 61, Dissenters' Cemetery and Chapel |
| VALLIS WAY | Nos 4, 5, 6, 7, 8, 8a, 9, 10, 31, and 39 |
| VICARAGE STREET | The Churchyard Gatepier, *St John's Vicarage,* Nos 15, 23, 24, 25, 26, 27, 28 and 33 |
| WALLBRIDGE | The Bridge, Nos 7, 8, 9, 10 and 11, and Wallbridge Mills |
| WELSHMILL ROAD | Bromstone, Garth, *Mendip House, Welshmill House,* Welshmill Lodge |

| | |
|---|---|
| **WESLEY SLOPE** | The Methodist Church, The Church Hall, Nos 1, 1a, 2, The School and No 3 |
| **WEYMOUTH ROAD** | The Former Selwood Hospital main block, lodge, tramps' room, etc. |
| **WHITEMILL LANE** | Knoll House |
| **WHITTOX LANE** | Nos 6, 9, 10, 11, 12, *Melrose House,* Zion United Reformed Church, The Sunday School |
| **WILLOW VALE** | Nos 1,2, 3, The Maltings, Nos 4, 5, 5a, Millhouse Court, The Dye-house, Willow Vale House, The Willows, *Nos 14, 15 and 16* |
| **WILTSHIRE'S BARTON** | *Nos 1, 2 and 3* |
| **WINE STREET** | Nos 3, 20, *No 21,* Nos 24 and 25 |

For confirmation, up-dating and for further details, the full list should be consulted: copies may be seen at the offices of the Frome Town Council, (in Palmer Street), or at the Mendip District Council Offices (Planning & Amenities Department) at Shepton Mallet. Be warned that there are some minor errors in the compilation of the list.

# INDEX

143

147

148